SCHOLASTIC
studySMART

Comprehension Skills

Level 6
English

◾SCHOLASTIC
Welcome to studySMᐧRT !

Comprehension Skills provides opportunities for structured and repeated practice of specific reading skills at age-appropriate levels to help your child develop comprehension skills.

It is often a challenge to help a child develop the different types of reading skills, especially as she encounters an increasing variety of texts. The age-appropriate and engaging texts will encourage your child to read and sift out the important information essential to read specific kinds of texts. As your child progresses through the levels, she will encounter a greater variety of skills and texts while continuing to practice previously learnt skills at a more difficult level to ensure mastery.

Every section targets a specific reading skill and the repeated practice of the skill ensures your child masters the reading skill. There are extension activities that can be done for specific reading skills to encourage your child to delve even deeper into the texts.

How to use this book?

1. Introduce the target reading skill at the beginning of each section to your child.

2. Let your child complete the reading exercises.

3. Reinforce your child's learning with an extension activity at the end of each activity. These activities provide additional practice, and extend your child's learning of the particular reading skill.

Note: To avoid the awkward 'he or she' construction, the pronouns in this book will refer to the female gender.

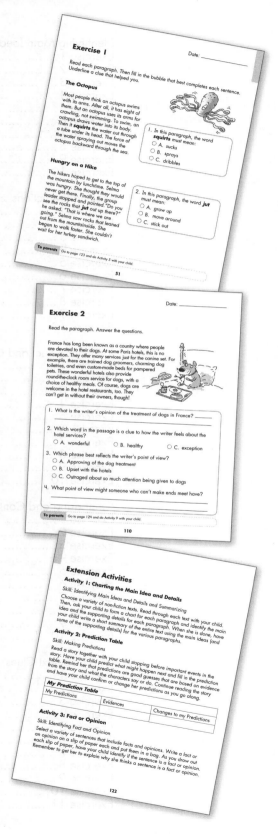

3

Contents

Identifying Main Ideas and Details

Reading comprehension involves numerous thinking skills. Identifying main ideas and the details that support them is one such skill. A reader who is adept at identifying main ideas makes better sense of a text and increases her comprehension of what is being communicated. The passages and questions in this section will help your child learn to recognize main ideas and the details that develop them.

Understanding the main idea of a passage is to be able to have a broad overall understanding of what a passage is all about. This section will provide opportunities for your child to understand that supporting details fill in information about the main idea and that the main idea is bigger and broader than the supporting details.

The extension activities provide additional challenges to your child to encourage and develop her understanding of the particular comprehension skill.

Exercise 1

Read each paragraph. Then fill in the bubble that best completes each sentence.

New Words

Dictionary writers are always busy. That's because the English language keeps changing. People stop using some words, and new words keep popping up. Where do new words come from? Many recent words are from technology. For example, *snailmail* came into use after people started using the much faster e-mail. Other new words come from books, television, movies and fads. Do you know what a *wannabe* is? If not, you can look it up in a recently published dictionary.

1. The main idea of this paragraph is:
   - ☑ A. Dictionaries show changes in the English language.
   - ○ B. How television affects English
   - ○ C. Why dictionary writers are so tired
   - ○ D. How to find new words in a dictionary

2. A supporting detail is:
   - ○ A. Snails help to deliver the mail.
   - ☑ B. Many words come from technology.
   - ○ C. Old dictionaries are not useful.
   - ○ D. The English language never changes.

To parents Go to page 122 and do Activity 1 with your child.

Exercise 2

Read each paragraph. Then fill in the bubble that best completes each sentence.

Building the Largest Jet Airliner

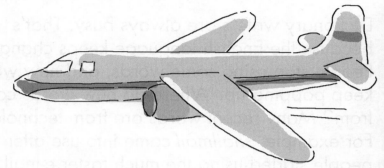

Where do you build the world's largest jet airliner? First, you have to put up the world's largest building. That's just what happened in Everett, Washington. An airplane factory there covers more than 98 acres under one roof. More than 75 NFL football fields could fit inside. More than 15 railcars a day deliver parts to the factory. Workers use overhead cranes and forklifts to assemble the large pieces. Buyers from all over the world purchase the finished airplanes.

1. The main idea of this paragraph is:
   - ○ A. Looking for the largest jet airliner
   - ○ B. The largest building is a jet factory.
   - ◉ C. Railcars deliver parts to the factory.
   - ○ D. How to build airplanes indoors

2. A supporting detail is:
   - ○ A. Choosing a place to build a factory
   - ○ B. Teams play football in the building.
   - ○ C. Visitors can tour the huge factory.
   - ◉ D. The factory covers about 98 acres.

To parents Go to page 122 and do Activity 1 with your child.

Exercise 3

Read each paragraph. Then fill in the bubble that best completes each sentence.

Father's Day

What is the history of Father's day? This holiday was first suggested by Sonora Smart Dodd in the early 1900s. She told her idea to people in her hometown of Spokane, Washington, and they began celebrating it. However, the holiday did not spread, and by the 1920s it had died out. Then in 1938 some men's clothing stores began promoting Father's Day as a way to raise sales. They used the slogan "Give Dad Something to Wear." In 1972, Father's Day finally became a national holiday in the U.S.

1. The main idea of this paragraph is:
   - ○ A. Giving clothes on Father's Day
   - ○ B. A national holiday in 1972
   - ○ C. The holiday that died out
   - ☑ D. A history of Father's Day

2. A supporting detail is:
   - ○ A. A family holiday in June
   - ○ B. Why fathers wear fashionable clothes
   - ☑ C. Sonora Smart Dodd first suggests the idea of Father's Day
   - ○ D. Send greeting cards on Father's Day

To parents Go to page 122 and do Activity 1 with your child.

Exercise 4

Read each paragraph. Then fill in the bubble that best completes each sentence.

Happy New Year

Happy New Year! People say this all over the world. However, not everyone celebrates this day in the same way. In Iceland, New Year's Eve is a time to clean up trash and perform elf dances. Families in Ecuador dance around scarecrows and read lists of people's faults. Later, when they set the scarecrow on fire, both it and the faults go up in flames. In Belgium, children write down good deeds they hope to perform. Chinese and Japanese get off to a good start by paying off all their debts. How do you celebrate the New Year?

1. The main idea of this paragraph is:
   - ○ A. Performing good deeds in Belgium
   - ○ B. How Americans celebrate the New Year
   - ✓ C. New Year's traditions around the world
   - ○ D. A time to pay off debts

2. A supporting detail is:
   - ○ A. How to celebrate the New Year
   - ○ B. January 1 is a national holiday
   - ○ C. Learning to do elf dances
   - ✓ D. Icelanders clean up trash

To parents Go to page 122 and do Activity 1 with your child.

Exercise 5

Read each paragraph. Then fill in the bubble that best completes each sentence.

The Oscars

If you are a movie fan, you have probably watched the Oscars on television. These awards for excellence in the film industry were first given in 1929. At that time there was no TV. Instead, 250 people attended a banquet in Hollywood sponsored by the Academy of Motion Picture Arts and Sciences. The winning film that year was *Wings*, a war story. As for the name Oscar, a secretary at the academy said the statue looked like her Uncle Oscar.

1. The main idea of this paragraph is:
   - ○ A. How the Oscars were named
   - ○ B. What movie fans do
   - ⊘ C. The first Oscar awards
   - ○ D. *Wings* won the first film award.

2. A supporting detail is:
   - ○ A. How to win an Oscar award
   - ⊘ B. The first Oscars were awarded in 1929.
   - ○ C. Watching the Oscars on television
   - ○ D. Why the Oscars are popular

To parents Go to page 122 and do Activity 1 with your child.

Exercise 6

Read each paragraph. Then fill in the bubble that best completes each sentence.

The Birthday Song

You turn a year old, and friends sing a certain song to you. The story of "Happy Birthday" goes back to the 1890s. In 1893 a teacher named Patty Smith Hill and her sister Mildred published a book called *Song Stories for Kindergarten*. The first song in the book was a four-line verse called "Good Morning to All." Patty soon wrote new words to this ditty, and it became the popular "Happy Birthday" song still sung today. People sing it in many languages around the world.

1. The main idea of this paragraph is:
   - ○ A. Celebrating birthdays
   - ○ B. Kindergarten songs
   - ○ C. The story of "Happy Birthday"
   - ○ D. A worldwide birthday song

2. A supporting detail is:
   - ○ A. Mildred Hill was a church organist.
   - ○ B. Patty Hill wrote the words.
   - ○ C. Kindergartners like to sing.
   - ○ D. People in Nepal sing the song.

To parents Go to page 122 and do Activity 1 with your child.

Exercise 7

Read each paragraph. Then fill in the bubble that best completes each sentence.

Henry Bergh and the ASPCA

In the 1860s an American named Henry Bergh was in Russia working for the U.S. government. He was horrified when he saw local peasants beating their horses in the streets. Soon after that, Bergh founded an organization in the United States to help animals. It was called the American Society for the Prevention of Cruelty to Animals (ASPCA). As the first president, Bergh worked hard to keep people from abusing animals. He even started an ambulance service for horses. It began two years before there was one for people.

1. The main idea of this paragraph is:
   ○ A. What Bergh saw in Russia
   ○ B. The life story of Henry Bergh
   ○ C. The first horse ambulance
   ⊘ D. How the ASPCA was started

2. A supporting detail is:
   ⊘ A. Bergh was the first president of the ASPCA.
   ○ B. Horses pulled carriages and wagons.
   ○ C. Bergh was a wealthy man.
   ○ D. The ASPCA still exists.

To parents   Go to page 122 and do Activity 1 with your child.

Exercise 8

Read each paragraph. Then fill in the bubble that best completes each sentence.

Foods in the Americas

When the first English settlers arrived in America, they were amazed at the foods they found. The Indians had developed techniques for growing corn, squash, watermelons and other crops. The settlers also found blueberries, cranberries, wild rice and pumpkin. They learned to eat lobster and crab as well as cod and striped bass. Still other foods included nuts such as cashews, black walnuts, hickory nuts and pecans. Wild turkeys were also a first for the settlers.

1. The main idea of this paragraph is:
   - ⊘ A. Local foods found by English settlers
   - ○ B. How Indians caught seafood
   - ○ C. A variety of new nuts to eat
   - ○ D. Berries were plentiful

2. A supporting detail is:
   - ○ A. A new menu for the settlers
   - ○ B. The settlers ate their first turkey.
   - ○ C. Kidney and lima beans were good.
   - ⊘ D. Native foods were delicious.

To parents   Go to page 122 and do Activity 1 with your child.

Exercise 9

Read each paragraph. Then fill in the bubble that best completes each sentence.

Calendars

Not everyone in the world uses the same calendar. If you are a Hindu, you follow the Hindu calendar. It has 360 days divided into 12 months of 30 days each. The months are counted from full moon to full moon. A leap month is added every five years to the keep the calendar in line with the seasons. Each month has two parts; Krsna is the first part, when the moon is getting smaller, and Sukla is the second part, when the moon is getting fuller. Some names of months are Chaitra, Asadha and Pausa.

1. The main idea of this paragraph is:
   - ○ A. Calendars around the world
   - ○ B. The two parts of a Hindu month
   - ☑ C. Understanding the Hindu calendar
   - ○ D. A year of 12 months

2. A supporting detail is:
   - ○ A. Chaitra is one Hindu month
   - ○ B. Special Hindu holidays
   - ☑ C. How to name the Hindu months
   - ○ D. Kinds of Hindu calendars

To parents Go to page 122 and do Activity 1 with your child.

Exercise 10

Read each paragraph. Then fill in the bubble that best completes each sentence.

Favorite Stones

Have you ever carried a stone around in your pocket? According to a tradition of the Seneca, a favorite stone can tell something about you. If your stone is smooth, it means you are gentle. A rough stone means that you follow creative ideas. Gray stones suggest that you are friendly, while brown ones mean you love nature. The shape of your stone has meaning too. A round stone says you are flexible. Is your stone oval? You are seeking a better life.

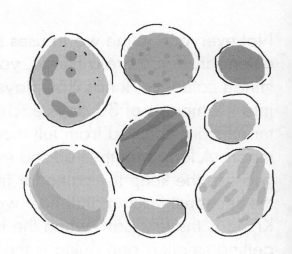

1. The main idea of this paragraph is:
   - ○ A. It's good to carry stones in your pockets.
   - ○ B. Stones are previous possessions.
   - ○ C. Rough stones mean creativity.
   - ◐ D. Stones have meaning to the Seneca.

2. A supporting detail is:
   - ○ A. Everyone should carry a stone.
   - ◐ B. Brown stones mean you love nature.
   - ○ C. Stones are found in many colors.
   - ○ D. A stone's shape is not important.

To parents Go to page 122 and do Activity 1 with your child.

Making Predictions

Making predictions is one of the many essential reading skills that young readers need to have. A reader who can think ahead to determine what may happen next or how an event may turn out gains a richer understanding of a text. The passages and questions in this section will help your child learn to make reasonable predictions and anticipate probabilities.

This section will provide opportunities for your child to guess what is likely to happen based on information which he or she already knows as well as the information in the text.

The extension activities provide additional challenges to your child to encourage and develop her understanding of the particular comprehension skill.

Exercise 1

Read each paragraph. Then fill in the bubble that best answers each question.

Cape Town

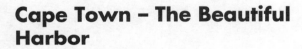

Cape Town is the oldest city in South Africa. It is an important trading port where ships traveling across the Indian Ocean and Atlantic Ocean stop to load and unload their cargoes and replenish their supplies. Because of its pleasant climate, it is also a popular vacation spot for people all over the country.

1. Which sentence tells what most likely happens next?
   - ○ A. Holiday makers will stroll in the lovely parks in Cape Town.
   - ⦿ B. Cape Town will import and export different types of goods.
   - ○ C. Cape Town will welcome migrants from all over the world.

Cape Town – The Beautiful Harbor

Alex watched quietly as the seagulls glided gracefully just above the water and the ships drifted effortlessly in the harbor. The big orange sun, moving slowly towards the ocean, added to the majesty of the scene right before his eyes. "What a picturesque view," he thought to himself, "if only I could capture this moment on my canvas."

2. Which sentence tells what most likely happens next?
   - ○ A. He will go for dinner.
   - ○ B. He will take out some bread to feed the seagulls.
   - ⦿ C. He will take out his paintbrush and paint the scene before him.

To parents   Go to page 122 and do Activity 2 with your child.

Exercise 2

Read each paragraph. Then fill in the bubble that best answers each question.

The Youngest Queen

Mary Stuart was declared queen of Scotland when she was barely a week old. Mary's father, King James of Scotland, died shortly after receiving the devastating news that the Scots were defeated by the English at war. As the English and the Scots were constantly at war, Mary was sent to France at the age of five to keep her safe.

1. Which sentence tells what most likely happens next?
   - ○ A. Mary will grow up to enjoy singing and dancing.
   - ✓ B. Mary will become a powerful queen later in her life.
   - ○ C. Mary will marry French royalty.

The Wise Queen

Queen Anna was well loved by her subjects. She was regal and compassionate, but most importantly, she was wise. Once, a married couple went to seek her counsel; they had lost a cow and suspected their neighbor of stealing it. They had no evidence to prove the cow that turned up overnight at their neighbor's backyard was theirs.

2. Which sentence tells what most likely happens next?
   - ○ A. Queen Anna will ask the couple to buy another cow.
   - ○ B. Queen Anna will ask the couple and their neighbor questions about caring for cows.
   - ✓ C. Queen Anna will tell the couple and their neighbor to sell the cow and share the proceeds.

To parents Go to page 122 and do Activity 2 with your child.

Exercise 3

Read each paragraph. Then fill in the bubble that best answers each question.

Why Onions Make Us Cry

Every time we blink, our eyes produce tears to cleanse our cornea and prevent them from drying out. When irritants attack our eyes, our eyes react by making tears to wash them out. Onions produce an oil that contains sulphur. This is the substance that gives the onion its sharp, tangy odor. However, this same substance also irritates our eyes.

1. Which sentence tells what most likely happens next?
   ○ A. This substance makes onions more nutritious.
   ⊘ B. When we cut an onion, we will cry.
   ○ C. When we cut an onion, we will stop blinking.

Cutting an Onion

"Mom is crying in the kitchen," whispered Nick to Priscilla. "Did you do anything to make her sad?" Priscilla put down her book and asked her little brother. Nick thought about it for a moment and shook his head firmly. The children tiptoed to the door of the kitchen quietly. Indeed, Mom was cutting rapidly and sniffing loudly.

2. Which sentence tells what most likely happens next?
   ⊘ A. The children will see Mom cutting an onion.
   ○ B. The phone will ring.
   ○ C. Mom will turn around and shout, "Surprise!"

To parents   Go to page 122 and do Activity 2 with your child.

Exercise 4

Read each paragraph. Then fill in the bubble that best answers each question.

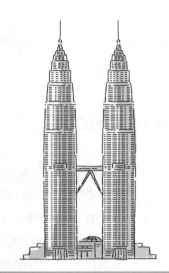

Who is the Tallest?

The race to the sky is common in modern day society. From the Petronas Towers in Malaysia to Taipei 101 in Taiwan, the race to build the tallest skyscraper in the world never stops. Since ancient times, big buildings have been used to show off power and wealth. They are also used to honor leaders or religious beliefs.

1. Which sentence tells what most likely happens next?
   - ⊘ A. People will continue competing to build the tallest building.
   - ○ B. More concrete will be used to build tall buildings.
   - ○ C. More skyscrapers will be built next to each other.

The Sky is the Limit

Grandpa lifted his head to see the gigantic building towering over him. It was beyond his wildest imagination. He had no idea where the skyscraper would stop. "Can man really reach the sky?" Grandpa mused silently. Things were unlike what they used to be when he was a boy. Everyone back then lived in simple wooden houses.

2. Which sentence tells what most likely happens next?
   - ○ A. Grandpa will not dare to take the elevator.
   - ○ B. Grandpa will lose his way.
   - ✓ C. Grandpa will tell his grandchildren all about the past.

To parents   Go to page 122 and do Activity 2 with your child.

Exercise 5

Read each paragraph. Then fill in the bubble that best answers each question.

Haute Couture

Haute couture is the business of designing, creating and selling high fashion women's clothes. It is costly and time consuming to make haute couture clothing. Each piece of clothing is made from scratch and tailor made to suit the whims and fancies of its buyer. It usually requires three fittings and takes about 100 to 400 hours to make a dress.

1. Which sentence tells what most likely happens next?
   - ○ A. Designers will loan clothes to movie stars for publicity.
   - ○ B. More and more people will be able to afford haute couture.
   - ⦸ C. Only rich people will be able to afford haute couture.

Dolly's New Dress

Jana looked closely at her doll, Dolly. Something was wrong. Her dress seemed ragged; a button had fallen off from the front of her dress and the side pocket had been ripped off by the family cat. It was time to make Dolly some new clothes. Jana ransacked through her Mum's sewing bag. She found some scrap pieces of cloths. One of them could be made into a dress for Dolly.

2. Which sentence tells what most likely happens next?
   - ○ A. Jana will sew back the button on Dolly's dress.
   - ⦸ B. Jana will make Dolly a new dress.
   - ○ C. Jana will scold the family cat.

To parents Go to page 122 and do Activity 2 with your child.

Exercise 6

Read each paragraph. Then fill in the bubble that best answers each question.

Arabian Nights

Did you know that stories could save lives? According to a legend, queen Scheherazade, a prisoner of Sultan Schahriah, would tell him intriguing tales each night. However, she would stop at the most exciting part so that he would have to wait until the next night to learn what happened. After 1,001 nights, the sultan spared her life. She later became his wife, and her stories were recorded down in books.

1. Which sentence tells what most likely happens next?
   - ○ A. Scheherazade will tell the stories to her friends.
   - ☑ B. People today will continue to enjoy the stories that Scheherazade told the king.
   - ○ C. The Sultan will find someone else to tell him stories.

Reading Corner

Mrs Hudson told her class to bring in some storybooks to share with one another. She wondered what kinds of books her students would bring. Kylie brought in her favorite fantasy novels. She really enjoyed reading the Harry Potter series. Ian showed his classmates his collection of books ranging from murder mysteries to horror stories.

2. Which sentence tells what most likely happens next?
   - ○ A. The children will go to the library.
   - ○ B. Mrs Hudson will tell her class stories.
   - ☑ C. The children will be excited to share their books.

To parents Go to page 122 and do Activity 2 with your child.

Exercise 7

Read each paragraph. Then fill in the bubble that best answers each question.

AIDS

AIDS (Acquired Immune Deficiency Syndrome) is a virus that may have developed as long as 50 to 150 years ago, but was not identified until 1981. It destroys the body's immune system and hence its ability to fight illnesses. The AIDS virus may take years to produce symptoms in an infected human being. AIDS patients can be located all over the world.

1. Which sentence tells what most likely happens next?
   - ○ A. AIDS will continue to spread throughout the world.
   - ○ B. People will become immune to AIDS.
   - ○ C. Less people will develop AIDS in the future.

Coughing

David hated to be sick. The idea of consulting someone in a white robe, with a snake-like stethoscope around his neck sent shivers down his neck. David could feel his coughs coming. He tried to stifle them but failed miserably. His coughs came strong and mighty, like the rainstorm that hit the city last night. Mom glanced at David with a frown on her face.

2. Which sentence tells what most likely happens next?
   - ○ A. David will go out in the rain.
   - ○ B. David will get better.
   - ○ C. Mom will take David to the doctor.

To parents Go to page 122 and do Activity 2 with your child.

24

Exercise 8

Read each paragraph. Then fill in the bubble that best answers each question.

Leonardo da Vinci

Leonardo da Vinci was born on 15 April, 1452 in Vinci, Italy. Even as a young boy, Leonardo was very curious and imaginative. He would painstakingly observe plants, animals and how things work, all the time making sketches and asking himself questions. He also loved to design things and is known not just as one of the great artists. Many people have studied his works.

1. Which sentence tells what most likely happens next?
   - ○ A. He will become very rich.
   - ○ B. He will become friends with many people.
   - ☑ C. His inventions and designs will be studied by people even today.

Painting

Amy loved to paint. She had always wanted to be a painter. She loved to be able to express her ideas, thoughts and feelings on paper; something she could not do very well in speech. Her eyes lit up whenever she saw paintings she liked. She particularly admired Claude Monet's paintings; paintings that create lasting impressions in the minds of viewers.

2. Which sentence tells what most likely happens next?
   - ○ A. Amy will learn to speak well.
   - ○ B. Amy will visit Claude Monet's water garden in France.
   - ☑ C. Amy will take painting lessons.

To parents Go to page 122 and do Activity 2 with your child.

Exercise 9

Read each paragraph. Then fill in the bubble that best answers each question.

Popsicles

Do you know that some foods were discovered by accident? The popsicle was one of them. In 1905, Frank Epperson, an eleven year old boy, was mixing powdered soda and water to make soda pop. He accidentally left the mixture out in the cold. During the night, the mixture became frozen, with the wooden stirring stick standing straight up. The frozen pop was delicious and refreshing!

1. Which sentence tells what most likely happens next?
   - ○ A. Frank will throw away the popsicle.
   - ✓ B. Frank will start selling Epperson icicles.
   - ○ C. Frank will develop more deserts.

Orange Marmalade

It was a bright and cheery afternoon. Carey and Mum were busy making orange marmalade for Carey's school funfair. They peeled the skins off the oranges and removed the seeds. After that, they cut the oranges into small pieces. Mum then put the cut oranges and half a kilogram of sugar into a big pot.

2. Which sentence tells what most likely happens next?
   - ✓ A. Mum will cook the mixture over a low heat, stirring from time to time.
   - ○ B. Mum will put the pot into the oven.
   - ○ C. Mum will tell Carey to complete her homework.

To parents Go to page 122 and do Activity 2 with your child.

Exercise 10

Read each paragraph. Then fill in the bubble that best answers each question.

Animation

You might be familiar with cartoons by the Walt Disney company, with the colorful characters, music and moving images. Before we had animated movies however, there were books called kineographs. These books had pages with a series of images printed near the edge of the page. When the reader flips through the book quickly, the images create an illusion of an animated scene or character. These days, if people want to see moving images, they watch an animated movie.

1. Which sentence tells what most likely happens next?
   - ○ A. Kineographs will become popular again.
   - ○ B. Kineographs will take over animated movies as a form of entertainment.
   - ✓ C. Animated movies will continue to wow audiences all over the world.

Moving Images

Candice was excited. The new animated movie is going to be shown on screen. She has been waiting for it the whole school term. After class, she headed down to the nearest cinema with her friend, Kyle. As they approached the cinema, they saw a long snaking queue.

2. Which sentence tells what most likely happens next?
   - ✓ A. The tickets will be sold out and they will watch the movie another time.
   - ○ B. They will run out of money.
   - ○ C. They will watch the movie that day.

To parents   Go to page 122 and do Activity 2 with your child.

Identifying Fact and Opinion

Being able to identify and distinguish between a fact and an opinion is an important reading comprehension skill, especially as readers start to encounter a variety of texts. A reader who can differentiate between statements of fact and opinion are better able to analyze and assess a text. The passages and questions in this section will help your child learn to identify statements of fact and opinion.

This section will provide opportunities for your child to understand that a fact can be proved to be true, while an opinion is what someone thinks or believes and is a kind of judgment.

The extension activities provide additional challenges to your child to encourage and develop her understanding of the particular comprehension skill.

Exercise 1

Read the paragraph. Follow the instructions.

In Britain, judges and lawyers have traditionally worn wigs and gowns in court. Depending on their role, some also wear lace neck trimmings, sashes, hoods, fur mantles and buckled shoes. From time to time, this judicial finery has been mocked. After all, it is ridiculous. The curly wigs are made in four shades of off-white, ranging from light gray to beige. The more important the official, the fancier the wig. A senior judge wears a headpiece of curls that reaches to the shoulders. What a silly, fussy, dusty custom!

1. Write *fact* or *opinion* next to each sentence.

   __Fact__ A. In Britain, judges and lawyers have traditionally worn wigs and gowns in court.

   __Fact__ B. From time to time, this judicial finery has been mocked.

   __Opinion__ C. What a silly, fussy, dusty custom!

2. Write another fact from the paragraph. _A Senior judge wears a head piece of curls that reaches to his/her shoulders._

3. Write another opinion from the paragraph. _After all, it is ridiculous_

To parents   Go to page 122 and do Activity 3 with your child.

Exercise 2

Date: _____

Read the paragraph. Follow the instructions.

Most surfers find their waves in the ocean, but in Brazil, surfers find them in the Amazon River. Each March and April, strong tides from the Atlantic Ocean push into the Amazon basin. These tides create a giant swell that travels upstream for hundreds of miles at speeds of 20 miles per hour. Brazilians call this endless wave a *pororoca*. Surfing for miles up the river is much more fun than a short ocean ride. All surfers should try this unique challenge.

1. Write *fact* or *opinion* next to each sentence.

   ___Fact___ A. Brazilians call this endless wave a *pororoca*.

   ___Opinion___ B. All surfers should try this unique challenge.

   ___Fact___ C. These tides create a giant swell that travels upstream for hundreds of miles at speeds of 20 miles per hour.

2. Write another fact from the paragraph. _Each March and April strong tides push up onto the Amazon Basin._

3. Write another opinion from the paragraph. _Surfing for miles is more fun than the ocean._

To parents Go to page 122 and do Activity 3 with your child.

Exercise 3

Read the paragraph. Follow the instructions.

A feature of many modern houses is the Palladian window. This window, with its three panels and curved top, takes its name from the architect Andrea Palladio. He lived in the sixteenth century in Italy. That was an excellent time for talented people. Palladio studied the architecture of the ancient Romans. No one could build like the Romans. During his lifetime, Palladio designed villas, churches and other public buildings. Visitors to Italy can still see many of these buildings today.

1. Write *fact* or *opinion* next to each sentence.

   _____ A. A feature of many modern houses is the Palladian window.

   _____ B. No one could build like the Romans.

   _____ C. Visitors to Italy can still see many of these buildings today.

2. Write another fact from the paragraph. _____

   _____

   _____

3. Write another opinion from the paragraph. _____

   _____

   _____

To parents   Go to page 122 and do Activity 3 with your child.

Exercise 4

Read the paragraph. Follow the instructions.

People have been living with domesticated animals for thousands of years. For example, dogs and people go back about 14,000 years. Believe me, dogs are "man's best friend". Cats have been around for a long time too. The ancient Egyptians thought of cats as gods. People should remember that because most cats today think of themselves as gods! Both children and adults should have pets. Birds, rabbits and some types of fish are popular pets. They're not as satisfying as dogs and cats, though.

1. Write *fact* or *opinion* next to each sentence.
   _____ A. Both children and adults should have pets.
   _____ B. The ancient Egyptians thought of cats as gods.
   _____ C. Believe me, dogs are "man's best friend".

2. Write another fact from the paragraph. _____
   _____
   _____

3. Write another opinion from the paragraph. _____
   _____
   _____

To parents   Go to page 122 and do Activity 3 with your child.

Exercise 5

Read the paragraph. Follow the instructions.

In Korea, people mark a child's first birthday with a celebration called *tol*. One this occasion, it is believed that babies pick their future. The child sits at a table covered with different objects. If the child picks a string, it means a long life. Everyone should pick that. If a baby picks money or rice, it indicates a business career. A musical instrument means the child will become an artist. That's a good choice. A special rice-cake soup is served at *tol* celebrations. I think cake and ice cream are better.

1. Write *fact* or *opinion* next to each sentence.

   _____ A. The child sits at a table covered with different objects.

   _____ B. Everyone should pick that.

   _____ C. A special rice-cake soup is served at *tol* celebrations.

2. Write another fact from the paragraph. _____

   _____

   _____

3. Write another opinion from the paragraph. _____

   _____

   _____

To parents   Go to page 122 and do Activity 3 with your child.

Exercise 6

Read the paragraph. Follow the instructions.

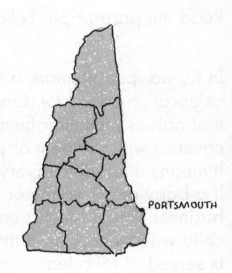

PORTSMOUTH

You should visit Strawbery Banke in Portsmouth, New Hampshire. This is a settlement that is now an outdoor history museum. Parts of Strawbery Banke were built in the 1600s; others are more recent. Visitors can see how people lived during three centuries in American history. It's really interesting. The guides dress as people did during each period. They act as if they were living during that time. They make barrels, pottery, baked goods and other things. You'll enjoy this place.

1. Write *fact* or *opinion* next to each sentence.

   _____ A. You should visit Strawbery Banke in Portsmouth, New Hampshire.

   _____ B. Parts of Strawbery Banke were built in the 1600s, others are more recent.

   _____ C. It's really interesting.

2. Write another fact from the paragraph. _____

   _____

   _____

3. Write another opinion from the paragraph. _____

   _____

   _____

To parents   Go to page 122 and do Activity 3 with your child.

Exercise 7

Read the paragraph. Follow the instructions.

Eartha is the world's largest moving globe. If you see it, you'll feel a sense of wonder. Eartha is more than 41 feet in diameter and weighs about 5,600 pounds. It rotates just like planet Earth. It was developed from computer technology and is made from one of the largest mapping databases in the world. To visit Eartha, you have to go to Yarmouth, Maine. The globe is housed in a three-story glass building there. It's very impressive.

1. Write *fact* or *opinion* next to each sentence.

   _____ A. If you see it, you'll feel a sense of wonder.

   _____ B. It rotates just like planet Earth.

   _____ C. To visit Eartha, you have to go to Yarmouth, Maine.

2. Write another fact from the paragraph. _____

   _____

   _____

3. Write another opinion from the paragraph. _____

   _____

   _____

To parents   Go to page 122 and do Activity 3 with your child.

Exercise 8

Read the paragraph. Follow the instructions.

Many living things have internal clocks. These are daily patterns known as circadian rhythms. One of the most common is the pattern of sleep that humans follow. Certain flowers have patterns, too. These flowers open and close their petals on specific schedules. For example, dandelions open at nine in the morning. People should get rid of dandelions because they're weeds. A morning glory opens at 10 a.m. and a water lily at 11. My favorite flower is the California poppy. Its petals open at 1 p.m.

1. Write *fact* or *opinion* next to each sentence.

    _____ A. Many living things have internal clocks.

    _____ B. My favorite flower is the California poppy.

    _____ C. For example, dandelions open at nine in the morning.

2. Write another fact from the paragraph. _____

    _____

    _____

3. Write another opinion from the paragraph. _____

    _____

    _____

To parents   Go to page 122 and do Activity 3 with your child.

Date: _____

Exercise 9

Read the paragraph. Follow the instructions.

A good way to spend free time is by playing games. During the
Civil War (1861–1865), both Union and Confederate soldiers
had time between battles. So the troops amused themselves in
different ways. The Union soldiers played a popular board
game called "The Checkered Game of Life". It was such a
terrific game! Whoever invented it must have
been very clever. A version of this game is still
around today. It is now called "The Game of
Life". Have you ever played it?

1. Write *fact* or *opinion* next to each sentence.

_____ A. The Union soldiers played a popular board game
called "The Checkered Game of Life".

_____ B. A good way to spend free time is by playing games.

_____ C. It was such a terrific game!

2. Write another fact from the paragraph. _____

_____

_____

3. Write another opinion from the paragraph. _____

_____

_____

To parents   Go to page 122 and do Activity 3 with your child.

Exercise 10

Read the paragraph. Follow the instructions.

Email is short for electronic mail. Many of us would be familiar with the term now as it has become a very convenient and popular way of communicating with other people. Emails are a really fantastic invention. They are easy to use as you can save them on your computer as well. Emails are fast. They are delivered straight away to someone else's email account. They are also environmentally friendly as you don't need paper to send an email. You can even send pictures in them. More people should use emails to communicate.

1. Write *fact* or *opinion* next to each sentence.

   _____ A. Emails are a fantastic invention.

   _____ B. Emails are fast.

   _____ C. They are environmentally friendly as you don't need paper to send an email.

2. Write another fact from the paragraph. _____

   _____

   _____

3. Write another opinion from the paragraph. _____

   _____

   _____

To parents   Go to page 122 and do Activity 3 with your child.

Comparing and Contrasting

Making comparisons is an essential reading comprehension skill that enriches a reader's understanding of the text. A reader who can compare and contrast events, characters, places, and facts is able to identify similarities and differences, and to categorize or group information. The passages and questions in this section will help your child learn to compare and contrast.

This section will provide opportunities for your child to understand that comparing and contrasting helps him or her to organize and comprehend information in the text. This is essential especially as your child encounters more nonfiction texts.

The extension activities provide additional challenges to your child to encourage and develop her understanding of the particular comprehension skill.

Exercise 1

Read the paragraph. Then answer the questions.

Green Fingers

Jake's flower patch looked like a rainbow. He couldn't wait for the seasonal flowers to be in full bloom. It would be such a welcome sight. From the window next door, Ken admired Jake's lush lawn. Both had been tending the garden all summer. Ken sighed as he stared at his own front porch. It was weedy and patchy-brown. All his potted plants were so sad-looking. He did a lot on the garden, but perhaps he just didn't have green fingers. He decided to walk across to Jake's for coffee. Since they had always been good neighbors, Ken decided to ask Jake for some gardening tips.

1. How are Jake and Ken similar?

   ○ A. They both worked hard on their gardens all summer.

   ○ B. They both had a lovely front garden.

   ○ C. They both love gardening.

2. How are Jake and Ken different?

   ○ A. Jake likes coffee.

   ○ B. Jake is a good gardener.

   ○ C. Ken knows how to grow a thick green lawn.

3. Write another way that Jake and Ken are alike.

   _____

   _____

   _____

   _____

   _____

   _____

To parents Go to page 123 and do Activity 4 with your child.

40

Exercise 2

Read the paragraph. Then answer the questions.

Dolphins and Porpoises

As dolphins and porpoises are very similar, they are often misidentified by people. Both dolphins and porpoises are marine mammals. They live in oceans, rivers and estuaries and are extremely intelligent. They have large, complex brains and generate sound waves to help them navigate in the water. Dolphins and porpoises feed on fish. The main difference is that dolphins are more talkative and love to interact with people. They make whistling sounds through their blowholes to communicate with one another. In comparison, porpoises tend to be timid and shy.

1. How are dolphins and porpoises alike?

   ○ A. They live on land and in the water.

   ○ B. They are both intelligent marine mammals.

   ○ C. They are friendly creatures.

2. How are dolphins and porpoises different?

   ○ A. Dolphins are more friendly.

   ○ B. Porpoises feed on fish.

   ○ C. Dolphins have large brains.

3. Write another way that dolphins and porpoises are alike.

   _____

   _____

   _____

   _____

   _____

To parents Go to page 123 and do Activity 4 with your child.

Date: _____

Exercise 3

Read the paragraph. Then answer the questions.

Two Musical Geniuses

Beethoven and Mozart are two great musical composers from the 18th century. Mozart was born in Austria in 1756 and was known as a child prodigy. He was playing short music pieces at four and began composing music when he was five. Like Mozart, Beethoven has been admired as a composer. He was born into a family of musicians in Germany in 1770. However, Beethoven did not show real talent until he was much older. He also had a unique problem; he started to lose his hearing when he was just a child. Thus, he wrote beautiful music from his memory of the sounds of music.

1. How are Beethoven and Mozart alike?
   - ○ A. They were child prodigies.
   - ○ B. They are both born into families of musicians.
   - ○ C. They are both admired for their skills as composers.

2. How are Beethoven and Mozart different?
   - ○ A. Beethoven is deaf.
   - ○ B. Mozart is deaf.
   - ○ C. Beethoven was born in the 18th century.

3. Write another way that Beethoven and Mozart are different.

   _____
   _____
   _____
   _____
   _____
   _____

To parents Go to page 123 and do Activity 4 with your child.

42

Exercise 4

Read the paragraph. Then answer the questions.

Allergies

Hay fever and hives are allergic reactions that make people miserable. Hay fever is an allergic reaction to pollen from weeds, grass or trees. It is common during spring. People who suffer from hay fever sneeze repeatedly, have watery eyes and runny noses. On the other hand, people who suffer from hives have itchy red patches and blisters on the body, which may sting and burn. Hives are caused by an allergic reaction to certain foods like milk, shellfish, berries and nuts. Insect bites can also cause hives.

1. How are hay fever and hives alike?
   - ○ A. They are common during spring.
   - ○ B. They are allergic reactions.
   - ○ C. Allergic reaction to food causes hay fever and hives.

2. How are hay fever and hives different?
   - ○ A. People with hives have itchy rashes and blisters.
   - ○ B. Hives make people miserable.
   - ○ C. Hay fever can happen to adults as well as children.

3. Write another way that hay fever and hives are different.

   _____

   _____

   _____

   _____

   _____

   _____

To parents Go to page 123 and do Activity 4 with your child.

Exercise 5

Read the paragraph. Then answer the questions.

Entertainers of the Middle Ages

Minstrels and jesters are entertainers of the Middle Ages. Minstrels sang and played songs telling of great battles, honor and chivalry. They played many different musical instruments. Most traveled around the country performing at castles or manors. Jesters, however, usually stayed in the same place and served the same lord. A jester was a medieval comedian. His job was to entertain his master and make him laugh. He wore funny, brightly colored clothes and performed tricks like juggling, acrobatic stunts, and other comedic feats. He was also expected to be witty with words.

1. How are minstrels and jesters alike?

   ○ A. They are entertainers of the Middle Ages.

   ○ B. They are street performers.

   ○ C. They traveled around the country.

2. How are minstrels and jesters different?

   ○ A. Minstrels performed at castles and manors.

   ○ B. Minstrels are witty with words.

   ○ C. Jesters entertained their masters.

3. Write another way that minstrels and jesters are different.

   _____

   _____

   _____

   _____

   _____

To parents   Go to page 123 and do Activity 4 with your child.

Exercise 6

Read the paragraph. Then answer the questions.

Butterflies and Moths

Both butterflies and moths are winged insects with a pair of antennae. Although butterflies and moths may look similar, they are quite different. Unlike butterflies that are diurnal and are active during the day, moths are nocturnal. Most butterflies have brightly colored wings. Moths are usually plain brown, grey, white or black which help camouflage them during the day. When at rest, moths spread out their wings but butterflies frequently fold their wings above their backs. Moth caterpillars spin a cocoon made of silk but butterflies form a chrysalis during their process of metamorphosis.

1. How are butterflies and moths alike?

   ○ A. They spin cocoons.

   ○ B. They have dully colored wings.

   ○ C. They undergo a process of metamorphosis.

2. How are butterflies and moths different?

   ○ A. Butterflies are insects.

   ○ B. Moths are nocturnal but butterflies are diurnal.

   ○ C. Moths have antennae.

3. Write another way that butterflies and moths are alike.

   _____

   _____

   _____

   _____

   _____

To parents   Go to page 123 and do Activity 4 with your child.

Exercise 7

Read the paragraph. Then answer the questions.

Weapons Across the Eras

Compared to modern weaponry, people in the past battled simple weapons they made themselves using wood, stone or iron. Primitive men broke branches of trees to make clubs. However, a club had its limitations as the enemy had to be nearby. They also used other weapons such as slings and bows. Modern day weapons have greater destructive power. Men nowadays use weapons such as rifles, rocket bombs and grenades. They do not have to be close to their enemies to create mass destruction. Missiles and bombs can be fired from a long distance and can cause a lot of damage and fatalities.

1. How are primitive weapons and modern day weapons alike?

   ○ A. They are used to attack enemies.

   ○ B. Enemies have to be nearby.

   ○ C. They are very destructive.

2. How are primitive weapons and modern day weapons different?

   ○ A. Modern day weapons are made of wood and stone.

   ○ B. Primitive weapons can be fired from far.

   ○ C. Modern day weapons have great destructive power.

3. Write another way that primitive weapons and modern day weapons are different.

   _____

   _____

   _____

   _____

   _____

To parents   Go to page 123 and do Activity 4 with your child.

Exercise 8

Read the paragraph. Then answer the questions.

Fables or Fairy Tales?

Fables and fairy tales are stories enjoyed by people throughout the ages. Fables are written for adults and children, while fairy tales are written specially for children. Fables are told to teach a lesson about something. Animals, plants and forces of nature are often personified in fables. They are given human qualities. The famous Aesop's Fables, were written by a man named Aesop. Fairy tales, on the hand, often include magical characters such as elves, fairies and giants. Sometimes the characters can be animals too. The Grimm Brothers are famous for writing fairy tales such as "The Frog Prince" and "Cinderella".

1. How are fables and fairy tales alike?

   ○ A. They are told to teach a lesson about something.

   ○ B. They are written for children.

   ○ C. They are written by Aesop.

2. How are fables and fairy tales different?

   ○ A. Fairy tales often include magical creatures.

   ○ B. Fables are written for children.

   ○ C. Fairy tales are written for adults.

3. Write another way that fables and fairy tales are alike.

   _____

   _____

   _____

   _____

   _____

To parents Go to page 123 and do Activity 4 with your child.

Exercise 9

Read the paragraph. Then answer the questions.

Lions versus Tigers

Lions and tigers are both ferocious animals but there are vital differences between them. They belong to the cat family and have no predators of their own. Lions typically inhabit the savanna and grasslands, although they may take to the forest. They are unusually sociable compared to other cats. Most female lions hunt together in the daytime. The male lion is easily recognized by its distinctive mane. Native to the mainland of Asia, the tiger is the largest feline species in the world. They are recognized by the black stripes all over their bodies. They usually hunt alone at night. Both lions and tigers are endangered, with the majority of the world's tigers now living in captivity.

1. How are lions and tigers alike?
   ○ A. They are both social animals.
   ○ B. They are both endangered.
   ○ C. They are both herbivores.

2. How are lions and tigers different?
   ○ A. Female tigers hunt in groups.
   ○ B. Male lions have manes.
   ○ C. Male tigers have manes.

3. Write another way that lions and tigers are alike.

   _____

   _____

   _____

   _____

   _____

To parents   Go to page 123 and do Activity 4 with your child.

Exercise 10

Read the paragraph. Then answer the questions.

Kangaroos and Wallabies

Kangaroos and wallabies are sure to make you think of Australia, because that is where they live. Both kangaroos and wallabies are classified as marsupials and carry their young in their pouches. However, wallabies and kangaroos are very different in size. Kangaroos are much bigger and taller. Their strong legs are made to hop quickly across open land while wallabies are more nimble in forested areas where they stay. Wallabies are brighter in color compared to the dull-colored kangaroos. Both wallabies and kangaroos are herbivores but the shape and size of their teeth are very different because of the different kinds of plants they eat.

1. How are wallabies and kangaroos alike?

   ○ A. They both eat meat.

   ○ B. They are both endangered.

   ○ C. They are both marsupials.

2. How are wallabies and kangaroos different?

   ○ A. Wallabies have longer legs.

   ○ B. Kangaroos are much more dully colored.

   ○ C. Wallabies carry their young in their pouches.

3. Write another way that wallabies and kangaroos are different.

   _____

   _____

   _____

   _____

   _____

   _____

To parents Go to page 123 and do Activity 4 with your child.

Using Context Clues

Being able to use context clues to make accurate estimations of unfamiliar words or phrases is essential in helping a reader better understand what is being communicated in a text. Very often, writers may use words that are unfamiliar to readers. However, there are often clues in the rest of the text to point to what that word means. Readers need to be able to sift out those clues to make sense of the text. The passages and questions in this section will help your child learn to use contextual clues to understand difficult or unfamiliar vocabulary.

This section will provide opportunities for your child to understand that using contextual clues means to look at the rest of the passage to try and figure out what a particular word or phrase means. This is especially the case when the writer does not explicitly provide the definition of the word in the passage because that would interrupt the flow of the passage. This is important as your child encounters a variety of texts and writing styles.

The extension activities provide additional challenges to your child to encourage and develop her understanding of the particular comprehension skill.

Exercise 1

Read each paragraph. Then fill in the bubble that best completes each sentence. Underline a clue that helped you.

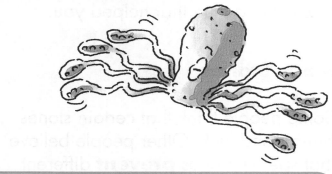

The Octopus

Most people think an octopus swims with its arms. After all, it has eight of them. But an octopus uses its arms for crawling, not swimming. To swim, an octopus draws water into its body. Then it **squirts** the water out through a tube under its head. The force of the water spraying out moves the octopus backward through the sea.

1. In this paragraph, the word **squirts** must mean:
   ○ A. sucks
   ○ B. sprays
   ○ C. dribbles

Hungry on a Hike

The hikers hoped to get to the top of the mountain by lunchtime. Selma was hungry. She thought they would never get there. Finally, the group leader stopped and pointed. "Do you see the rocks that **jut** out up there?" he asked. "That is where we are going." Selma saw rocks that leaned out from the mountainside. She began to walk faster. She couldn't wait for her turkey sandwich.

2. In this paragraph, the word **jut** must mean:
   ○ A. grow up
   ○ B. move around
   ○ C. stick out

To parents   Go to page 123 and do Activity 5 with your child.

Exercise 2

Read each paragraph. Then fill in the bubble that best completes each sentence. Underline a clue that helped you.

Stone Stories

Some people think that certain stones bring good luck. Other people believe that special stones **prevent** different problems. For example, diamonds are thought to keep away nightmares. Garnets are supposed to keep people free from injury. Pearls and jade are thought to keep wearers from harm.

1. In this paragraph, the word **prevent** must mean:
   - ○ A. to keep from happening
   - ○ B. to cause trouble
   - ○ C. to make believe

Randy's Art

Randy spent a lot of time drawing. Her teacher, Miss Begay, looked at Randy's pictures. They were good. Randy had a real **flair.** "Why don't you enter some pictures in the school art show?" Miss Begay said. At first Randy wasn't sure, but finally she entered three pictures. Best of all, one of her pictures won a prize.

2. In this paragraph, the word **flair** must mean:
   - ○ A. talent
   - ○ B. flame
   - ○ C. prize

To parents   Go to page 123 and do Activity 5 with your child.

Exercise 3

Read each paragraph. Then fill in the bubble that best completes each sentence. Underline a clue that helped you.

All About Trees

Suppose you are lost in a forest. You might find your way by looking at the trees. **Observe** them carefully. The side of a tree with the most leaves and branches is the south side. The tops of trees lean toward the south too. If you study the bark closely, you'll see that it is lighter and brighter on one side. That is also the south side. But if you see moss at the base of a tree, it will be on the north side.

1. In this paragraph, the word **observe** must mean:
   - ○ A. circle
   - ○ B. ignore
   - ○ C. examine

New Rollerblades

The first time that Clay tried out his rollerblades, he learned an important lesson. Parts of the sidewalk were not very good for skating. In these places the sidewalk was bumpy and **uneven**. Clay found that it was much easier to keep his balance on smooth sections.

2. In this paragraph, the word **uneven** must mean:
   - ○ A. unfair
   - ○ B. not straight
   - ○ C. not level

To parents Go to page 123 and do Activity 5 with your child.

Exercise 4

Read each paragraph. Then fill in the bubble that best completes each sentence. Underline a clue that helped you.

Writing About Pippi

Sometimes writers have trouble getting started. They **stall** for time. For example, Astrid Lindgren couldn't make herself write about Pippi Longstocking for a long time. Then she hurt her ankle and had to stay at home. Lindgren couldn't put off her work anymore. She began her book.

1. In this paragraph, the word **stall** must mean:
   - ○ A. trade
   - ○ B. start
   - ○ C. delay

Honey at Home

Cara's cat didn't like to be left alone. Cara never knew what Honey would do when the family was out. Sometimes the cat just slept. But sometimes she was bad. One day Cara found a big mess in the bathroom. Honey had unrolled the toilet paper. It was in **shreds**. Bits of it were everywhere. It took a long time to clean up Honey's mess.

2. In this paragraph, the word **shreds** must mean:
   - ○ A. rolls
   - ○ B. pieces
   - ○ C. squares

To parents   Go to page 123 and do Activity 5 with your child.

54

Exercise 5

Read each paragraph. Then fill in the bubble that best completes each sentence. Underline a clue that helped you.

What Happened?

Why did dinosaurs disappear? Scientists have different ideas. One possible idea is that there was a long **drought** during the time of dinosaurs. This dry period caused changes in the plants that grew on Earth. These changes meant that the dinosaurs didn't have enough sources of food to live.

1. In this paragraph, the word **drought** must mean:
   ○ A. stormy season
   ○ B. period without rain
   ○ C. cloud of dust

The Town Parade

Each year there was a parade in Marco's town. The night before, people blew up huge balloons. They decorated floats. The bands practiced their music. Marco wanted to see all this activity. His mother said he should wait and see the parade. Marco began to **plead**. He asked his mother over and over until she agreed.

2. In this paragraph, the word **plead** must mean:
   ○ A. beg
   ○ B. praise
   ○ C. march

To parents Go to page 123 and do Activity 5 with your child.

Exercise 6

Read each paragraph. Then fill in the bubble that best completes each sentence. Underline a clue that helped you.

Dr Blackwell

Elizabeth Blackwell was the first woman doctor in the United States. She became a doctor in 1849. At that time no hospital would hire a woman in this role. So Elizabeth Blackwell started her own hospital. As a doctor, she had a big **concern**. She was interested in helping people to live in healthier conditions. Dr Blackwell worked hard to help make this happen.

1. In this paragraph, the word **concern** must mean:
   - ○ A. care or interest
   - ○ B. kind of work
   - ○ C. large office

Bad Idea

The campers thought it would be fun to play a **prank** on their counselor. They decided to put salt in his toothpaste. However, Bud did not think this joke was funny. He made the campers use the salty toothpaste every night for a week.

2. In this paragraph, the word **prank** must mean:
   - ○ A. game
   - ○ B. trick
   - ○ C. flavor

To parents   Go to page 123 and do Activity 5 with your child.

Exercise 7

Read each paragraph. Then fill in the bubble that best completes each sentence.
Underline a clue that helped you.

Recycling

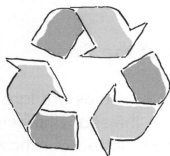

We can help to save our environment by
recycling. Recycling helps prevent our landfills
from filling up with waste products too rapidly.
Landfills can **pollute** our environment and
underground water nearby. In addition,
recycling also helps to preserve our natural
resources. Although some natural resources
such as forests can be grown, it takes a long
time for it to flourish. Therefore, it is necessary
for us to use our resources carefully.

1. In this paragraph, the word
   pollute must mean:
   ○ A. dirty
   ○ B. beautify
   ○ C. fill

Lantern Design Contest

David and his sister were busy collecting
empty boxes, used containers, unwanted
buttons and materials. They were planning
to **participate** in this year's lantern design
contest organized by their school. The theme
of this year's contest was to use unwanted
materials to create lanterns. David decided
to make a car using empty boxes and paper
plates. His sister would make a giraffe with
toilet rolls and buttons.

2. In this paragraph, the word
   participate must mean:
   ○ A. excited
   ○ B. take part
   ○ C. cross

To parents   Go to page 123 and do Activity 5 with your child.

Date: _____

Exercise 8

Read each paragraph. Then fill in the bubble that best completes each sentence. Underline a clue that helped you.

Giants of the Seas

Humpback whales are large mammals that live in the sea. Like humans, they are warm-blooded and have a body temperature of 37 degrees Celsius. They do not have gills and have to swim to the surface of the water to take in air. Humpback whales breathe through their nostrils called blowholes. They can use up to 90% of the oxygen they take in. Because of their **efficiency** in breathing, they can stay underwater for as long as 30 minutes.

1. In this paragraph, the word **efficiency** must mean:
   ○ A. ability to swim
   ○ B. ability to do something well
   ○ C. ability to finish a task

Ring .... Ring ....

Ring … ring…the alarm rang as usual. Cedric pulled his blanket tightly over his head. He refused to get up. He was feeling **lethargic** and did not want to go to school. He wanted to stay at home and laze around. Cedric could hear his mother's footsteps approaching. He had to think quickly of an excuse not to go to school.

2. In this paragraph, the word **lethargic** must mean:
   ○ A. excited
   ○ B. dejected
   ○ C. tired

To parents Go to page 123 and do Activity 5 with your child.

Exercise 9

Read each paragraph. Then fill in the bubble that best completes each sentence. Underline a clue that helped you.

Remembrance Day

At the eleventh hour of the eleventh day of the eleventh month of each year, Canadians everywhere observe Remembrance Day. This day **commemorates** the brave ones who answered the call of duty and died in wars or on peace-keeping missions. In schools, some teachers and students display wartime postcards and telegrams of Canadian war heroes. Men and women also wear red poppies on their lapels as a symbol of remembrance.

1. In this paragraph, the word **commemorates** must mean:
   ○ A. honors
   ○ B. sneers
   ○ C. reserves

Only a Tail

Paul crouched down silently on the grass. He wanted to catch the lizard that was basking in the sun for his show and tell. He stretched out his hand slowly and caught hold of the lizard by its tail. Paul ran home quickly, eager to show his father his prized catch. When he reached home, he was surprised to see only a tail in his hand. Paul's father explained that a lizard has a special way of escaping from its enemy called **self-amputation**.

2. In this paragraph, the word **self-amputation** must mean:
   ○ A. cutting off part of its body
   ○ B. blending in with the surrounding
   ○ C. running away quickly

To parents Go to page 123 and do Activity 5 with your child.

Exercise 10

Read each paragraph. Then fill in the bubble that best completes each sentence. Underline a clue that helped you.

The Amazing Tree Bark

Though the bark of a tree may not be as **eye-catching** as its flowers or leaves, they are of great use to man. Ancient man wrote on birch bark using a sharp instrument. The bark of the evergreen cork oak is used to make cork. Sometimes tree bark is also used in food. The cinnamon that gives flavor to our food is scraped from the bark of the cinnamon tree while chewing gum is manufactured from the bark of the sapodilla.

1. In this paragraph, the word **eye-catching** must mean:
   - ○ A. catching an eye
   - ○ B. useful
   - ○ C. draws attention

Paw Prints

Jason and Jennifer were panting hard from their long walk up the hill. They had their backpacks and carried long sticks to feel their way through the thick undergrowth. As they were walking, they noticed a set of gigantic paw-prints. "Those prints might be made by a tiger prowling nearby," Jason whispered. They were **anxious**. Quickly and quietly, they started to make their way out of the jungle.

2. In this paragraph, the word **anxious** must mean:
   - ○ A. excited
   - ○ B. worried
   - ○ C. cross

To parents Go to page 123 and do Activity 5 with your child.

Date: _____

Exercise 11

Read each paragraph. Then fill in the bubble that best completes each sentence. Underline a clue that helped you.

How Clouds Are Formed

A cloud is a large collection of water droplets that are so tiny and light that they can float in the air. When warm air rises from the land or sea, it carries water vapor with it. At a higher altitude, the air gets colder. As cold air cannot hold as much water vapor as warm air, some of the vapor condenses and forms tiny droplets around dust particles. When billions of these droplets come together they become a **visible** cloud.

1. In this paragraph, the word **visible** must mean:
   ○ A. can be eaten
   ○ B. can be painted
   ○ C. can be seen

Our Story Clouds

My favorite pasttime was to lie under the big oak tree in our garden and look at the clouds in the sky. Sometimes, my sister Jody would join me in imagining what each cloud would be. Sometimes a cloud could be a majestic castle; at other times, a ferocious shark. Jody and I would take turns to **conjure** stories about the clouds. Our stories could range from romantic stories of a prince fighting a dragon to funny stories of a clown with an oversized hat. We had great fun.

2. In this paragraph, the word **conjure** must mean:
   ○ A. discuss
   ○ B. paint
   ○ C. invent

To parents Go to page 123 and do Activity 5 with your child.

Exercise 12

Read each paragraph. Then fill in the bubble that best completes each sentence. Underline a clue that helped you.

Black Death

The first outbreak of the bubonic plague (or Black Death) was recorded in 1331 in China. It was highly **contagious** and killed millions of people across parts of Asia, North Africa and Europe. The plague started as a bloody swelling in the armpit or groin and quickly invaded the whole body. It was carried by fleas which lived in the fur of the black rat. As the rats lived in close proximity to humans, the disease spread speedily.

1. In this paragraph, the word **contagious** must mean:
   ○ A. notorious
   ○ B. infectious
   ○ C. popular

Mr Wilkinson's Will

The children of the late Mr Wilkinson gathered in the living room, waiting for their father's will to be read. A stately man with a pair of black-rimmed glasses walked into the room. There was an immediate silence. Everyone looked **expectantly** at the man. He must be Mr Wilkinson's appointed lawyer. The man sat and started rummaging through his bag. He brought out a massive pile of documents and drew a business card from the pile. He was a property estate agent.

2. In this paragraph, the word **expectantly** must mean:
   ○ A. in disappointment
   ○ B. in anger
   ○ C. in anticipation

To parents   Go to page 123 and do Activity 5 with your child.

Exercise 13

Read each paragraph. Then fill in the bubble that best completes each sentence. Underline a clue that helped you.

Planets in the Solar System

Before the existence of telescopes, only five planets were visible. These planets were Mercury, Venus, Mars, Jupiter and Saturn. In 1608, an Italian astronomer, Galileo, built the first telescope. He did not find any new planets but **discovered** that Jupiter had moons. The seventh planet was discovered by William Herschet in 1781. He spotted a mysterious greenish object orbiting the sun and named it Uranus.

1. In this paragraph, the word **discovered** must mean:
   - ○ A. found something new
   - ○ B. made something new
   - ○ C. bought something

An Unusual Encounter

Farmer Brown was having a relaxing evening after a hard day's work. He was watching his favorite television show in his big, comfortable couch. Just when he was about to doze off, he heard a loud bang. He jumped to his feet immediately and rushed outside to the backyard. To his amazement, he saw a green saucer-like object lying there. It was **illuminated** in colorful, blinking lights.

2. In this paragraph, the word **illuminated** must mean:
   - ○ A. darkened
   - ○ B. lighted up
   - ○ C. blinded by

To parents Go to page 123 and do Activity 5 with your child.

Exercise 14

Read each paragraph. Then fill in the bubble that best completes each question.

Parasites

Parasites are plants or animals that live in or on a host (animal or plant). They get their nourishment from their host without killing them. Although parasites are normally **undesirable**, sometimes they can help the host animals. Some hermit crabs place sea anemones on their shells, hiding under their protective stinging tentacles. At the same time, sea anemones benefit because they share the crab's food.

1. In this paragraph, the word **undesirable** must mean:
   ○ A. unwelcome
   ○ B. popular
   ○ C. harmful

The Three Seeds

Once upon a time, three seeds were **scattered** by a gentle breeze. The first seed was carried to a rocky mountain and landed there. There was no soil and the seed withered under the scorching sun. The breeze blew on. The second seed went a little further. It landed on some soil. However, the weeds snatched away its nutrients so it could not grow. The breeze blew on. The last seed landed in a garden. This time, the seed grew to be a strong, beautiful flower under the nourishment of the fertile soil, rain and sunlight.

2. In this paragraph, the word **scattered** must mean:
   ○ A. destroyed
   ○ B. dispersed
   ○ C. blown

To parents Go to page 123 and do Activity 5 with your child.

Summarizing

Summarizing helps a reader identify the important points in a text and make sense of what is being communicated in a text. Very often, writers provide many details as examples of what they mean but these examples are not necessary in conveying the essential message in the passage. That is where summarizing is important. Readers are required to condense the information that they read and to restate the ideas in the text using their own words or phrases. By summarizing, readers learn to identify the main ideas and differentiate the essential information from the details. The passages and questions in this section will help your child learn to summarize a passage.

This section will provide opportunities for your child to read a text closely to pick out the central ideas in a text and understand which are the details supporting the text. They are then required to use the information they have sifted out to form a summary. This is important as your child encounters a variety of texts and various forms of communication.

The extension activities provide additional challenges to your child to encourage and develop her understanding of the particular comprehension skill.

Exercise 1

Read the paragraph. Answer the questions.

In 1588, the Spanish Armada sailed to fight against England. The armada consisted of a fleet of 130 ships. Aboard one of these ships was a tailless cat. Her job was to catch mice. After a great naval battle that England dominated, the Spanish ships set sail for home. The cat's ship was wrecked near the Isle of Man. The nimble cat got ashore safely and lived there ever after. Her many descendants became known as Manx cats after the name of their island home. Manx cats are known for being tailless.

1. What was unusual about the cat in the Spanish Armada?

   _____

2. What happened to the cat's ship?

   _____

3. Where did the cat end up living?

   _____

4. The title that best summarizes this paragraph is:
   - ○ A. Why Some Cats are Tailless
   - ○ B. Why the Spanish Lost at Sea
   - ○ C. How the Manx Cat Got Its Name
   - ○ D. Catching Mice Aboard a Ship

5. Use your answers to help you write a summary of the paragraph.

   _____

   _____

   _____

To parents Go to page 123 and do Activity 6 with your child.

Exercise 2

Read the paragraph. Answer the questions.

Some words are really combinations of two or more words. The new words are called blends. The meaning of a blend reflects the meanings of both words it comes from. For example, the words *gleam* and *shimmer* have been combined to make *glimmer*. The words *smoke* and *fog* blend to make *smog*. *Motor* and *cavalcade* combine to make *motorcade*. Can you figure out what *motor* and *hotel* make when combined? You're right — it's *motel*. What two words do you think *brunch* comes from?

1. What is a blend?

   _____

2. How does a blend get its meaning?

   _____

   _____

3. What are some examples of blends?

   _____

   _____

4. The title that best summarizes this paragraph is:
   - ○ A. Combining Smoke and Fog
   - ○ B. Learning About Blends
   - ○ C. How *Motel* Got Its Meaning
   - ○ D. Forming Compound Words

5. Use your answers to help you write a summary of the paragraph.

   _____

   _____

   _____

To parents Go to page 123 and do Activity 6 with your child.

Exercise 3

Read the paragraph. Answer the questions.

In 1638, a Swedish ship arrived in America. The immigrants aboard founded a community called Fort Christina. The Dutch soon took over this settlement but not before the Swedes had built snug log cabins like those in their homeland. The cabins were made of notched logs carefully fitted together without nails. The walls were chinked with moss or clay, and the roofs were made of hardwood. Plentiful lumber made these easy-to-build cabins ideal for settlers. Log cabins became a symbol of the pioneer spirit.

1. Who brought the log cabin to America?

_____

2. How were the cabins made?

_____

3. Why were they ideal for settlers?

_____

4. The title that best summarizes this paragraph is:

○ A. A Building Boom in 1638

○ B. Building the Pioneer Spirit

○ C. Contribution From the Dutch

○ D. Log Cabins from the Swedish

5. Use your answers to help you write a summary of the paragraph.

_____

_____

_____

To parents   Go to page 123 and do Activity 6 with your child.

Exercise 4

Read the paragraph. Answer the questions.

Buddy was the first seeing-eye dog in the United States. Despite the name, she was really a female. This German shepherd was trained at a place called Fortunate Fields in Switzerland in the 1920s. Then she was matched with a blind American named Morris Frank. He and Buddy learned to work together. When they returned to the United States, Frank started a school to train more guide dogs. It was called the Seeing Eye. Today, the school is in Morristown, New Jersey. It matches 300 blind people with dogs like Buddy each year.

1. Who was Buddy?

_____

2. Who was Morris Frank?

_____

3. What did Morris Frank start?

_____

_____

4. The title that best summarizes this paragraph is:
   ○ A. The First U.S. Seeing-Eye Dog
   ○ B. A Furry Gift From Switzerland
   ○ C. How Morris Frank Lost His Sight
   ○ D. Training at the Seeing Eye

5. Use your answers to help you write a summary of the paragraph.

_____

_____

_____

To parents Go to page 123 and do Activity 6 with your child.

Exercise 5

Read the paragraph. Answer the questions.

Most communities have laws about how high fences can be in residential neighborhoods. Why? One reason is safety. Fences that are too high can block the view of motorists in driveways or near intersections. Another reason is that people tend to argue about fences that neighbors put up, saying they are unattractive or made of ugly materials. Fences can also restrict the rights of others by blocking views, light or airflow. Good laws help settle such disputes.

1. How can fences be a safety problem?

   _____

2. How can fences irritate neighbors?

   _____

3. How can fences infringe on the rights of others?

   _____

4. The title that best summarizes this paragraph is:

   ○ A. Blocking Motorists' Views
   ○ B. Eliminating Ugly Fences
   ○ C. Building Fences in Neighborhoods
   ○ D. Why Communities Have Fence Laws

5. Use your answers to help you write a summary of the paragraph.

   _____

   _____

   _____

To parents   Go to page 123 and do Activity 6 with your child.

70

Exercise 6

Read the paragraph. Answer the questions.

The phrase *flotsam and jetsam* is often used to refer to the unfortunate in society. However, these words once referred to cargo found floating in water. Flotsam was cargo from a wrecked ship. Jetsam was cargo that was purposely thrown overboard either to lighten the ship's load or to keep the goods from going down with the ship. Jetsam belonged to the ship's owner. Anything that was flotsam belonged to the government.

1. What does *flotsam and jetsam* mean today?

   _____

2. What was flotsam?

   _____

   _____

3. What was jetsam?

   _____

   _____

4. The title that best summarizes this paragraph is:
   - ○ A. Society's Less Fortunate
   - ○ B. Story of Flotsam and Jetsam
   - ○ C. Learning About Flotsam
   - ○ D. Cargo From Shipwrecks

5. Use your answers to help you write a summary of the paragraph.

   _____

   _____

   _____

To parents   Go to page 123 and do Activity 6 with your child.

Exercise 7

Read the paragraph. Answer the questions.

When a hockey player scores three goals in a row with no other goals scored by other players, it is called a "hat trick". Where did this expression come from? It was originally used in the English game of cricket to describe a bowler taking three wickets on successive balls. The reward for such a feat was often a new hat. Sometimes fans passed a hat and took up a collection for the player who scored well. The term "hat trick" soon spread to other sports, including soccer and hockey.

1. What is a "hat trick" in hockey?

   _____

2. From what sport did the term come?

   _____

3. What do hats have to do with the term?

   _____

   _____

4. The title that best summarizes this paragraph is:
   ○ A. How to Score a Hockey Game
   ○ B. How Players Win Hats
   ○ C. The History of "Hat Trick"
   ○ D. Sports with "Hat Tricks"

5. Use your answers to help you write a summary of the paragraph.

   _____

   _____

   _____

To parents Go to page 123 and do Activity 6 with your child.

Exercise 8

Read the paragraph. Answer the questions.

Music was very popular with the armies during the Civil War. Soldiers on both sides liked to gather around campfires and sing familiar songs such as "Home! Sweet Home!" and "'Tis the Last Rose of Summer". Southerners often sang "Dixie", while Northerners favored "Yankee Doodle". A song written especially for the war was "Battle Hymn of the Republic" by Julia Ward Howe. The bugle melody "Taps" was also first played as a sign-off to a soldier's day during the Civil War.

1. What kinds of songs were popular during the Civil War?

   _____

2. What song was written for the war?

   _____

3. What other song was introduced during the war?

   _____

4. The title that best summarizes this paragraph is:
   - ○ A. Singing "Home! Sweet Home!"
   - ○ B. The First Use of "Taps"
   - ○ C. Music of the Civil War
   - ○ D. Why Soldiers Like to Sing

5. Use your answers to help you write a summary of the paragraph.

   _____

   _____

   _____

To parents   Go to page 123 and do Activity 6 with your child.

Exercise 9

Read the paragraphs. Answer the questions.

People take cars and other road vehicles for granted today. However, the idea of such vehicles was unheard of about 500 years ago. Then, in 1478, the artist and inventor Leonardo da Vinci designed a self-propelled vehicle. His drawing showed a boxy, open-topped wooden machine with three wheels. Coiled springs would make the vehicle move somewhat like a windup toy. Models of Leonardo's vehicle have been made in recent years and are on exhibit in museums in Italy.

1. What do people today take for granted?

   _____

2. What did da Vinci design in 1478?

   _____

3. How did his vehicle work?

   _____

   _____

4. The title that best summarizes this paragraph is:
   - ○ A. The Modern Car
   - ○ B. Da Vinci's Model Vehicle
   - ○ C. Cars 500 Years Ago
   - ○ D. Exhibits in Italian Museums

5. Use your answers to help you write a summary of the paragraph.

   _____

   _____

   _____

To parents   Go to page 123 and do Activity 6 with your child.

Exercise 10

Read the paragraph. Answer the questions.

Rattlesnakes are venomous reptiles that live in many places from southern Alberta in the United States of America to Central Argentina. They are brown, gray, or tan, and have diamond-shaped patches or bands on their bodies which serve as camouflage. Rattlesnakes do not have ears. They detect movement by sensing vibrations in the ground. Rattlesnakes have superb eyesight, even when it is dim. Their triangular heads contain hollow spots between the eyes and nostrils called pits. Pits help rattlesnakes hunt in darkness by detecting body heat. Rattlesnakes use their rattles, found at the tip of their tails, to warn their enemies or to distract prey.

1. What are rattlesnakes?

_____

2. How do they look like?

_____

_____

3. What are their rattles used for?

_____

_____

4. The title that best summarizes this paragraph is:
   ○ A. Camouflage
   ○ B. The Rattle
   ○ C. Rattlesnakes
   ○ D. Snakes in America

5. Use your answers to help you write a summary of the paragraph.

_____

_____

_____

To parents   Go to page 123 and do Activity 6 with your child.

Exercise 11

Read the paragraph. Answer the questions.

King Polydectes gave Perseus an almost impossible quest. He asked Perseus to bring back the head of Medusa, a dreadful creature with a head covered with poisonous snakes; anyone who looked at her would be turned into stone. Luckily, the gods gave Perseus a helmet which made him invisible, a shield that could act as a mirror, and a pair of shoes that enabled him to fly. When Perseus arrived at the island where Medusa lived, she was sleeping. He was able to behead Medusa with his sword by looking at her in his polished shield. The shield acted like a mirror and prevented Perseus from turning into stone.

1. What did Perseus have to do?

_____

2. Who helped Perseus?

_____

3. How did Perseus behead Medusa?

_____

_____

4. The title that best summarizes this paragraph is:
   - ○ A. The Quest of Perseus
   - ○ B. Medusa
   - ○ C. King Polydectes
   - ○ D. Greek Mythology

5. Use your answers to help you write a summary of the paragraph.

_____

_____

_____

To parents   Go to page 123 and do Activity 6 with your child.

Exercise 12

Read the paragraph. Answer the questions.

Marya Sklodowski loved reading. She could read for hours in intense concentration. One day, while the Sklodowski children were studying at the dining room table, the boarders decided to play a prank on Marya. They put a chair on each side of Marya's, and one behind her. Then they stacked two more chairs on top of the first three. Finally, they laid a chair on top of all the chairs, forming a pyramid of six chairs. Meanwhile, Marya was so focused on her reading that she was totally oblivious of the giggling children. However, when she attempted to leave the table, the pyramid of chairs came crashing down on her.

1. What were the Sklodowski children doing?

   _____

2. What prank did the boarders play on Marya?

   _____

   _____

3. What happened when Marya attempted to leave the table?

   _____

4. The title that best summarizes this paragraph is:
   - ○ A. A Prank on Marya Sklodowski
   - ○ B. The Prank
   - ○ C. Marya Sklodowski
   - ○ D. Life in a Boarding School

5. Use your answers to help you write a short summary of the paragraph.

   _____

   _____

   _____

To parents   Go to page 123 and do Activity 6 with your child.

Exercise 13

Read the paragraph. Answer the questions.

The International Red Cross and Red Crescent Movement is the largest humanitarian network in the world. It believes that humanity does not need to suffer, even in war. The symbol of the Red Cross is used to identify and protect people who give their time and compassion to help victims of war. Almost all the people who worked for the Red Cross and the Red Crescent Societies are volunteers. The Red Cross is always neutral. It does not take sides between warring countries or political parties. It helps people across the nations, without considering their political beliefs, wealth or social status.

1. What is the International Red Cross and Red Crescent Movement?

   _____

2. What is the symbol of the Red Cross used for?

   _____

   _____

3. Who does the Red Cross help?

   _____

4. The title that best summarizes this paragraph is:

   ○ A. The Red Cross and Red Crescent

   ○ B. Helping People Worldwide

   ○ C. A Humanitarian Organization

   ○ D. Volunteering in the Red Cross

5. Use your answers to help you write a summary of the paragraph.

   _____

   _____

   _____

To parents   Go to page 123 and do Activity 6 with your child.

Exercise 14

Read the paragraph. Answer the questions.

Bullying occurs when someone forces you to do things you are uncomfortable with, or does things to hurt you, make you feel afraid or depressed. Some bullies may demand that you tell lies, cheat, steal or do something dangerous for them. Others may threaten you, insult you or spread rumors about you. Some bullies may use physical force on children who are smaller than them to demonstrate their powers. Bullies succeed because their victims are too frightened to tell on them. Therefore if you are being bullied in school, it is important to let your teachers or parents know so that appropriate measures can be taken.

1. What is bullying?

   _____

2. What do bullies do?

   _____

   _____

3. What should you do if you are being bullied?

   _____

4. The title that best summarizes this paragraph is:
   - ○ A. Undesirable Social Behavior
   - ○ B. Physical Bullying
   - ○ C. Stop Bullying
   - ○ D. Bullying

5. Use your answers to help you write a summary of the paragraph.

   _____

   _____

   _____

To parents   Go to page 123 and do Activity 6 with your child.

Inferring

Making inferences is essential in helping a reader better understand what is being communicated in a text. Very often a text does not always include every fact or detail about a topic. Readers often draw upon their own knowledge or experiences to make sense of what is stated in a text. This process of mentally adding on information to aid comprehension is called inferring. The passages and questions in this section will help your child learn to make inferences.

This section will provide opportunities for your child to understand that inferring helps her fill in the information that is unstated and to make sense of a text. This is important as your child encounters a variety of texts and writing styles.

The extension activities provide additional challenges to your child to encourage and develop her understanding of the particular comprehension skill.

Exercise 1

Read the paragraph. Answer the questions.

Have you ever heard of a walking school bus? Students in some parts of the United States travel by such buses every day. The "driver" of these buses is often a parent who leads a group to and from school—on foot. If the group is large, there is usually another adult who walks at the end of the group to make sure everyone stays together. Students are picked up and dropped off at their homes. Walking buses help students get fresh air, and they also help reduce pollution and traffic congestion. Walking buses help students get fresh air, and they also help reduce pollution and traffic congestion.

SCHOOL CROSSING

1. Which sentences are most likely true?
   - ○ A. Walking school buses provide good exercise.
   - ○ B. Two adults would accompany a small group.
   - ○ C. Slow walkers could cause problems for a group.
   - ○ D. Walking buses may cause traffic jams.

2. Write *yes* or *no* under each heading on the chart to show if the word describes a walking school bus.

Healthy	Unsafe	Expensive

To parents Go to page 124 and do Activity 7 with your child.

81

Date: _____

Exercise 2

Read the paragraph. Answer the questions.

You've heard of recycling, but do you know about freecycling? When you freecycle, you give away things you no longer want or need. Freecyclers can also acquire things that someone else is getting rid of. Lists of things available for freecycling and lists of things wanted by freecyclers are posted on websites. People who sign up and find just what they want then arrange to pick up the items. Some popular items for freecyclers are bicycles, exercise equipment, furniture and computer parts.

1. Which sentences are most likely true?
   - ○ A. Freecycling is a good way to save money.
   - ○ B. People can also freecycle rubbish.
   - ○ C. Freecyling is convenient as it includes delivery.
   - ○ D. You could furnish a room from freecycled things.

2. Write *yes* or *no* under each heading on the chart to show if the word describes freecycling.

Costly	Dishonest	Useful

To parents   Go to page 124 and do Activity 7 with your child.

Exercise 3

Read the paragraph. Answer the questions.

NASCAR is the National Association for Stock
Car Racing. In recent years, this organization has
made some changes in its rules. For example,
steel and foam cushioning has been
placed around the NASCAR tracks
to better absorb impact from
hurting cars. Race car drivers must
now wear special head restraints that limit
their neck movement during sudden stops.
Air filters have been added to race cars to keep carbon monoxide out of the
cockpit. The tires also have straps now to keep the wheels from flying off
during crashes.

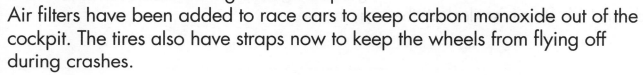

1. Which sentences are most likely true?
   ○ A. NASCAR's new rules were made to improve safety.
   ○ B. Car racing is a safe sport.
   ○ C. Anyone can be a race car driver.
   ○ D. Race car drivers can get seriously hurt.

2. Write *yes* or *no* under each heading on the chart to show if the word describe stock car racing.

Unregulated	Safety conscious	Dangerous

To parents   Go to page 124 and do Activity 7 with your child.

Exercise 4

Read the paragraph. Answer the questions.

When they come to a stoplight, drivers sometimes look at the people in other cars. Mr Beren noticed that a man in the car next to him had a large green parrot on the passenger seat. The parrot seemed to be talking. When the man rolled down his window, Mr Beren was surprised to hear that the bird wasn't talking but barking. The owner leaned out his window and explained, "He lives with three golden retrievers and he thinks he's a dog." The light changed, and Mr Beren smiled all the way home.

1. Which sentences are most likely true?
   ○ A. Mr Beren does not like parrots.
   ○ B. The driver in the other car amused Mr Beren.
   ○ C. The parrot learned to bark by listening to the dogs.
   ○ D. The parrot's behavior amused Mr Beren.

2. Write *yes* or *no* under each heading on the chart to show if the word describes Mr Beren's reaction.

Tickled	Disapproving	Uninterested

To parents   Go to page 124 and do Activity 7 with your child.

Exercise 5

Read the paragraph. Answer the questions.

Great Zimbabwe, a ruins located within the
African country of Zimbabwe, was a center
of trade from the late thirteenth century to the
middle of the fifteenth century. It was also the
home of powerful rulers. Today, scientists are
studying the walls found among the ruins. They
are made of smooth granite and are about
35 feet high and 16 feet high. No mortar
or plaster was used in building them. Some
archaeologists believe that the walls were built
not for defense but to inspire awe towards
the rulers.

1. Which sentences are most likely true?
   - ○ A. Great Zimbabwe is no longer part of Zimbabwe.
   - ○ B. Great Zimbabwe is a place of great historic value.
   - ○ C. The builders of the walls were skilled.
   - ○ D. Great Zimbabwe is no longer a center of trade.

2. Write *yes* or *no* under each heading on the chart to show if the word
   describes Great Zimbabwe.

Fascinating	Polluted	Ancient

To parents Go to page 124 and do Activity 7 with your child.

Exercise 6

Read the paragraph. Answer the questions.

During the Ice Age many, many thousands of years ago, people depended on the animals they hunted. Not only did they need these animals for food, but the hunters used them to make clothing, tools and other necessities. Ancient paintings found in caves show us what these animals were like. Some were huge, such as the woolly mammoth and the woolly rhinoceros. Other animals that inspired Ice Age artists still exist today. These include bison, horses, musk oxen and deer.

1. Which sentences are most likely true?

   ○ A. Some Ice Age animals are now extinct.

   ○ B. Animals were very important to Ice Age people.

   ○ C. Ice Age people were great admirers of art.

   ○ D. Horses and bison are animals that exist only today.

2. Write *yes* or *no* under each heading on the chart to show if the word describes life in the Ice Age.

Glamorous	Modern	Hard

To parents   Go to page 124 and do Activity 7 with your child.

Date: _____

Exercise 7

Read the paragraph. Answer the questions.

Prairie dogs are not really dogs; they're rodents. However, like canines, prairie dogs communicate by barking. Many of the sounds they make alert their colony to danger. For example, prairie dogs have one call for coyotes and another for hawks. When a coyote is sighted, other prairie dogs pop up from their burrows to keep track of where it goes. If a hawk is signaled, they dive into their burrows. Prairie dogs make other sounds when humans are near. Most surprisingly, prairie dogs have distinct calls for different kinds of real dogs.

1. Which sentences are most likely true?
   - ○ A. Prairie dogs belong to the dog family.
   - ○ B. Prairie dogs and coyotes get along very well.
   - ○ C. Hawks are bigger threats than coyotes.
   - ○ D. Prairie dogs have special calls for people.

2. Write *yes* or *no* under each heading on the chart to show if the word describes prairie dog communications.

Watchful	Unpleasant	Silent

To parents   Go to page 124 and do Activity 7 with your child.

Exercise 8

Read the paragraph. Answer the questions.

Many people put flowers in a vase, but in Japan arranging flowers is considered an art. It is called *ikebana* and has been practiced for about 500 years. Japanese teens often study flower arranging in school, and professional arrangers spend years learning the art. Only a few flowers are used in an arrangement. These are carefully chosen to make a graceful composition. The tallest flower represents heaven, the shortest flower is for earth, and the one in the middle stands for humans. Most homes in Japan have a special place where flower arrangements are displayed.

1. Which sentences are most likely true?
   - ○ A. Much thought goes into a Japanese flower arrangement.
   - ○ B. Ikebana is practiced all over the world.
   - ○ C. Ikebana reflects an appreciation of beauty.
   - ○ D. Ikebana uses many different flowers.

2. Write *yes* or *no* under each heading on the chart to show if the word describes ikebana.

Careless	Elegant	Meaningful

To parents Go to page 124 and do Activity 7 with your child.

Exercise 9

Read the paragraph. Answer the questions.

Did you know that monadnocks are inselbergs are similar? They are both landforms of isolated rock mountains that stand higher than a surrounding region. Because of their rock composition, monadnocks and inselbergs are not much affected by erosion. *Monadnock* is from a word in the Alogonquin language that was given to a mass of rock in New Hampshire called Mt Monadnock. The rock mountains called inselbergs tower above plains in tropical areas such as central Nigeria in Africa.

1. Which sentences are most likely true?
   - ○ A. Monadnocks have stayed the same for a very long time.
   - ○ B. Inselbergs and monadnocks occur in the same region.
   - ○ C. Monadnocks have a different appearance than other mountains.
   - ○ D. The Algonquins lived in what is now New Hampshire.

2. Write *yes* or *no* under each heading on the chart to show if the word describes monadnocks.

Unusual looking	Green	Level

To parents   Go to page 124 and do Activity 7 with your child.

Exercise 10

Read the paragraph. Answer the questions.

The organizers of the Olympics face many problems. One of the biggest is often the weather. In the years 1932, 1956, and 1964, a lack of snow made things difficult at the Winter Olympics. Scorching temperatures during some Summer Olympics have also caused problems. In 1924, only half of the runners in a cross-country event made it to the finish line because of the heat. Other weather-related problems have created headaches, too. In 1896 in Greece, the rowing races had to be cancelled because the sea was too rough. A flood once almost halted the Olympics in Paris.

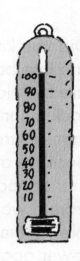

1. Which sentences are most likely true?
   - ○ A. The Olympic Games can only happen if there is good weather.
   - ○ B. Weather conditions have a big effect on the Olympic Games.
   - ○ C. Olympic organizers have to be good problem solvers.
   - ○ D. In the event of a lack of snow, the Winter Olympics will be cancelled.

2. Write *yes* or *no* under each heading on the chart to show if the word describes how weather affects the Olympics.

Unpredictable	Boring	Challenging

To parents   Go to page 124 and do Activity 7 with your child.

Date: _____

Exercise 11

Read the paragraph. Answer the questions.

It's fast, strong and a very good hunter. It can catch sand rats, jerboas and ground squirrels. It is also known for its jumping skills, which it uses when hunting birds. What is this animal? It's the caracal, a cat that lives in the deserts of Africa, the Middle East and parts of Asia. The caracal has short, sleek hair that is reddish-brown in color. Its large, pointed ears are black on the back. Usually, the caracal does its hunting at night to avoid the hot temperatures of the desert in daytime.

1. Which sentences are most likely true?
   - ○ A. The caracal runs very quickly to avoid predators.
   - ○ B. Temperatures in the desert drop at night.
   - ○ C. The caracal itself is a good predator.
   - ○ D. The caracal is nocturnal.

2. Write *yes* or *no* under each heading on the chart to show if the word describes the caracal.

Sweet	Predator	Fragile

To parents   Go to page 124 and do Activity 7 with your child.

Exercise 12

Read the paragraph. Answer the questions.

Long ago, there were no clocks or watches. People had to figure out ways to mark the passing of time. In about 870 A.D., King Alfred of England invented a candle clock. He used candles that were 12 inches long and marked them off in equal sections. To keep air drafts from affecting how the candle burned, he created a lantern to fit over the candle. People could then measure time by noting how long a section of the candle took to burn. The problem with candle clocks? They kept burning up!

1. Which sentences are most likely true?
   ○ A. The candle clock was a useful way of telling time in the past.
   ○ B. People had to keep replacing the candle clocks.
   ○ C. Candle clocks were not very useful.
   ○ D. England in 870 A.D. was probably very windy.

2. Write *yes* or *no* under each heading on the chart to show if the word describes the candle clock.

Clever	Permanent	Accurate

To parents Go to page 124 and do Activity 7 with your child.

Exercise 13

Read the paragraph. Answer the questions.

Emperor penguin parents share the responsibilities of caring for their offspring. The female lays one egg, which she places on the male's feet. He keeps the egg between the top of his feet and a special fold of skin on his tummy. He is careful not to drop the egg. While the female goes back to sea, the father huddles on the ice with other dads for two months. The males do not eat during this time. The female returns when the egg is ready to hatch. She feeds the chick a meal of fish. The male goes to find food in the sea for himself and the chick. Both parents then share the work of feeding the chick.

1. Which sentences are most likely true?
   ○ A. If the male drops the egg, the egg will hatch.
   ○ B. The female does not care about the young at all.
   ○ C. The male keeps the egg safe and warm.
   ○ D. The male is hungry by the time the chick hatches.

2. Write *yes* or *no* under each heading on the chart to show if the word describes penguin parents.

Impatient	Selfish	Dutiful

To parents   Go to page 124 and do Activity 7 with your child.

Drawing Conclusions

Being able to draw accurate conclusions from the information provided in a text helps is essential to help readers derive meaning from language with layers of implied meaning. The skill of drawing conclusions is related to that of making inferences, particularly when a text does not always state every bit of information explicitly. Readers often have to piece together the clues that the writer provides and then draw the best conclusions they can to understand the text. The passages and questions in this section will help your child learn to make inferences.

This section will provide opportunities for your child to understand that drawing conclusions helps him fill to use evidence in the text to come to make sense of text and to read between the lines. This is important as your child encounters a variety of texts and writing styles.

The extension activities provide additional challenges to your child to encourage and develop their understanding of the particular comprehension skill.

Date: _____

Exercise 1

Read the paragraph. Then fill in the bubble that best completes each sentence.

What's the secret of a winning cyclist? Skill, daring and good preparation do make a difference, of course, but another answer is technology. Since bicycle races are often very close, riders need every advantage they can get. For instance, a racer might wear a suit designed so that it has no creases or wrinkles to affect the airflow. Special racing shoes are covered with a seamless silver fabric for the same reason. Aerodynamic brakes and a bike frame made to cut through the air effectively are also part of a racer's equipment.

1. From this paragraph you can conclude that
   - ○ A. cyclists like to look good when racing.
   - ○ B. many riders wear the wrong kind of clothing.
   - ○ C. air resistance affects a rider's speed.
   - ○ D. some riders don't spend enough time training.

2. From the paragraph you cannot tell
   - ○ A. what materials are used in making racing bikes.
   - ○ B. that riders need every advantage they can get.
   - ○ C. that bicycle races are often very close.
   - ○ D. that riders must have skill to win a race.

To parents Go to page 124 and do Activity 8 with your child.

Exercise 2

Read the paragraph. Then fill in the bubble that best completes each sentence.

Elephants don't usually dress up, but some old clothing designers thought that these large animals could be quite fashionable. So the designers made some oversize outfits such as tweed suits, a cloak and some dresses. They even included gigantic earrings and shoes. The designers had to use stepladders to get their models dressed, but the elephants were very well behaved. When all was ready, a photographer took pictures for a fashion magazine. The money the elephants made from their modeling was donated to some elephant causes.

1. From this paragraph you can conclude that
   - ○ A. elephants enjoy reading fashion magazine.
   - ○ B. the clothing designers wanted to get attention.
   - ○ C. many people bought the elephant clothes.
   - ○ D. the elephants often work as fashion models.

2. From the paragraph you cannot tell
   - ○ A. how the elephants' earnings were used.
   - ○ B. why the designers made elephant clothes.
   - ○ C. what color clothes the elephants modeled.
   - ○ D. how the elephants acted when they were dressed.

To parents Go to page 124 and do Activity 8 with your child.

Exercise 3

Read the paragraph. Then fill in the bubble that best completes each sentence.

Most trees have leaves growing from their branches, but a cottonwood tree along U.S. Highway 50 near Middle Gate, Nevada, has something else. Hanging for the branches of this tree are shoes. High heels, work boots, flip-flops, baby booties, sandals, running shoes, even snorkeling flippers all dangle from this tree. Some people buy shoes just to put them in the tree. Other take them as needed. To the people who live in the area, the tree is a symbol of charity and decency. Many passersby have benefited from its unusual and useful offerings.

1. From this paragraph you can conclude that
   - ○ A. flip-flops are the most popular footwear in the tree.
   - ○ B. the shoes fall from the tree when autumn comes.
   - ○ C. people living nearby are proud of the tree.
   - ○ D. most of the shoes are worn and old and unusable.

2. From the paragraph you cannot tell
   - ○ A. where the cottonwood tree with shoes is located.
   - ○ B. why some of the shoes in the trees are new.
   - ○ C. what kinds of shoes are found in the tree.
   - ○ D. how the tradition of a tree with shoes got started.

To parents   Go to page 124 and do Activity 8 with your child.

Exercise 4

Read the paragraph. Then fill in the bubble that best completes each sentence.

When she was young, Madame C. J. Walker's hair began falling out. She tried a lot of remedies, but none helped. So she invented her own mixture – and it worked. Soon after, she decided to start her own hair-care business. At first, she sold her products door-to-door. Then she began selling products by mail. Madame Walker set up factories and opened beauty parlors in many cities. She also started training schools for her workers. By the time of her death in 1919, 25,000 women worked for Madame Walker. She was first black female millionaire. Much of her wealth went to help others.

1. From this paragraph you can conclude that

   ○ A. Madame C.J. Walker was a good businesswoman.

   ○ B. Madame Walker's products were very expensive.

   ○ C. no one used hair products before Madame Walker.

   ○ D. most hair products today are sold door-to-door.

2. From the paragraph you cannot tell

   ○ A. why Madame Walker invented a hair product.

   ○ B. what Madame Walker did with her money.

   ○ C. what ingredients were used in the hair products.

   ○ D. how Madame Walker sold her hair-care treatments.

To parents Go to page 124 and do Activity 8 with your child.

Exercise 5

Read the paragraph. Then fill in the bubble that best completes each sentence.

The Chinese learned to make silk cloth almost 5,000 years ago. At that time, they were the only ones who knew how to make it. Soon traders from China found that people in the West would pay great prices for silk. So traders traveled long distances on camels across harsh deserts and over high mountains to sell their silk. They also brought styles of art and Chinese inventions such as gunpowder to the West. They returned with gold, nuts, perfumes and goods from the West. This trade route became known as the Silk Route. Many of the stopping places on the route became great cities.

1. From this paragraph you can conclude that
   - ○ A. travel on the Silk Route was safe and easy.
   - ○ B. gunpowder was an unimportant Chinese invention.
   - ○ C. ideas were also exchanged along the Silk Route.
   - ○ D. prices charged in the West for silk were too high.

2. From the paragraph you cannot tell
   - ○ A. what kind of land the Silk Route crossed.
   - ○ B. the names of some of the cities along the Silk Route.
   - ○ C. what goods from the West traders brought to China.
   - ○ D. when the Chinese first began making silk.

To parents   Go to page 124 and do Activity 8 with your child.

Exercise 6

Read the paragraph. Then fill in the bubble that best completes each sentence.

What is letterboxing? It's a hobby that has grown in popularity in recent years. To get started you need a notebook, an ink pad, a compass and good walking shoes. Most people check a website to obtain clues telling how to find letterboxes.  Each letterbox is a container holding a rubber stamp and a notebook. Letterboxes are hidden in public places such as parks or woods. When seekers find a letterbox, they add its stamp to their notebook. Most letterbox fans also carry their own stamps, which they stamp into the notebook in the letterbox. This is called "stamping in".

1. From this paragraph you can conclude that
   - ○ A. everyone enjoys the hobby of letterboxing.
   - ○ B. letterboxing is an ancient tradition.
   - ○ C. people trespass a lot when letterboxing
   - ○ D. letterboxing is like an outdoor detective game.

2. From the paragraph you cannot tell
   - ○ A. what people will find in a letterbox.
   - ○ B. how many letterboxes exist in a particular place.
   - ○ C. where people go to find the clues for letterboxing.
   - ○ D. what equipment you need for letterboxing.

To parents   Go to page 124 and do Activity 8 with your child.

Exercise 7

Read the paragraph. Then fill in the bubble that best completes each sentence.

The phone at a zoo in Scotland kept ringing, but
no one spoke when the employees answered. The
only sound was a kind of snuffling noise. This went
on for two nights. Everyone was mystified. Then
an employee found the prankster. It was Chippy,
an 11-year-old chimp who had snatched a cell
phone from one of his keepers. To make his calls,
Chipy had been hitting the "redial" button. Thanks
to Chippy's cellular monkey business, the zookeeper's phone bill was rather high
that month! Since then, the keeper stores his cell phone in a deep pocket.

1. From this paragraph you can
conclude that

  ○ A. Chippy was playing with
the cell phone.

  ○ B. Chippy wanted to scare the
zoo employees.

  ○ C. Chippy wanted to pay for
the calls he made.

  ○ D. Chippy knew the telephone
number of the zoo.

2. From the paragraph you
cannot tell

  ○ A. how Chippy got the
cell phone.

  ○ B. how long Chippy had the
cell phone.

  ○ C. where the keeper stores his
phone now.

  ○ D. what other pranks Chippy
has pulled.

To parents   Go to page 124 and do Activity 8 with your child.

Exercise 8

Read the paragraph. Then fill in the bubble that best completes each sentence.

Passing motorists often think they have stumbled onto a huge art installation. Instead, they are going by a testing ground for a paint company. About 20,000 wood panels covered with paint and stain stand on a farm in New Jersey. The result is acres and acres of every shade of color. By leaving these panels out in each season and all kinds of weather, the company learns  how well and how long the paint holds up. Still, as one house painter points out, "No matter how good the paint is, you have to prepare the surface well first."

1. From this paragraph you can conclude that

   ○ A. yellow is the company's biggest seller.

   ○ B. the company is testing exterior paint.

   ○ C. the company also tests competitor's paint.

   ○ D. the paint panels are changed every month.

2. From the paragraph you cannot tell

   ○ A. what the company is hoping to learn.

   ○ B. where the testing grounds are located.

   ○ C. which colors hold up the best outside.

   ○ D. what you have to do first when painting.

To parents   Go to page 124 and do Activity 8 with your child.

Exercise 9

Read the paragraph. Then fill in the bubble that best completes each sentence.

What does it mean when you toss the salad? Most people think that's when you mix lettuce and dressing together. However, sanitation workers would say that tossing the salad means to throw garbage into the truck. Like workers in many fields, they have their own lingo. A garbage truck is known as a white elephant. Garbage that has been salvaged or saved by someone is called mongo. If a worker's job is to pick trash from street-corner cans, it is called running the baskets. As for the workers, they call themselves trash hounds.

1. From this paragraph you can conclude that
   - ○ A. people throw away a lot of salad.
   - ○ B. sanitation workers are fond of dogs.
   - ○ C. elephants are used for collecting garbage.
   - ○ D. lingo gives workers a sense of belonging.

2. From the paragraph you cannot tell
   - ○ A. what "running the baskets" means.
   - ○ B. there are two meanings for tossing the salad.
   - ○ C. how much garbage a truck collects.
   - ○ D. what salvaged garbage is called.

To parents Go to page 124 and do Activity 8 with your child.

Exercise 10

Read the paragraph. Then fill in the bubble that best completes each sentence.

Scientists have been learning more about ears. Until recently, most people thought both ears did the same work. However, studies have now shown that the right and left ear process sound differently. If you are listening to someone speaking, your right ear is responding. If you are listening to music, your left ear is more attuned. Researches think this new information is important in helping people with hearing loss. For example, a student with hearing loss in the right ear might need more help in school because the right ear is critical to learning situations.

1. From this paragraph you can conclude that
   - ○ A. people really don't need two ears.
   - ○ B. the left ear is important to musicians.
   - ○ C. the right ear is larger than the left ear.
   - ○ D. the left and right ear are interchangeable.

2. From the paragraph you cannot tell
   - ○ A. how scientists conducted their research.
   - ○ B. which ear processes speech best.
   - ○ C. who might benefit from this research.
   - ○ D. what people used to assume about ears.

To parents Go to page 124 and do Activity 8 with your child.

Exercise 11

Read the paragraph. Then fill in the bubble that best completes each sentence.

The Romans had a name for it. They called it "nomen et omen", meaning that names are a person's destiny. In other words, someone's name can determine what that person does. Researches who study this have come up with some convincing examples For example, Cecil Fielder was a baseball player. William Wordsworth was a famous poet. A well-liked weather reporter on television is Storm Field, and a popular entertainer is Tommy Tune. Larry Speakes was a presidential press secretary. Guess what David J Lawyer does!

1. From this paragraph you can conclude that
   - ○ A. everyone named Fish works in oceanography.
   - ○ B. all names relate to people's professions.
   - ○ C. someone named Rose might become a florist.
   - ○ D. a doctor named Kwak is not trustworthy.

2. From the paragraph you cannot tell
   - ○ A. who William Wordsworth was.
   - ○ B. the batting average of Cecil Fielder.
   - ○ C. what "nomen et omen" means.
   - ○ D. what kind of work Storm Field does.

To parents Go to page 124 and do Activity 8 with your child.

Exercise 12

Read the paragraph. Then fill in the bubble that best completes each sentence.

When Marco Polo visited China in the thirteenth century, he found many things that were new to him. He was amazed that people in China used paper money. This was unheard of in Europe at that time. Another surprise was the custom of bathing every day. In Europe, baths were taken very rarely, Even more amazing was the "black stone", or coal , used to heat the bath water. The wide streets of the city in which Kublai Khan, China's leader, lived also impressed Marco Polo. These streets were unlike the twisting, narrow lanes of Italy.

1. From this paragraph you can conclude that
   - ○ A. the Chinese printed their paper money in Europe.
   - ○ B. Europeans did not know much about China in the 1200s.
   - ○ C. people in the European countries took baths every day.
   - ○ D. Marco Polo was a ruler from Italy.

2. From the paragraph you cannot tell
   - ○ A. that Europeans were unfamiliar with paper money at the time.
   - ○ B. what the streets in Italy were like in the thirteenth century.
   - ○ C. what people in China found different about Marco Polo.
   - ○ D. who the leader of the Chinese was in the 1200s.

To parents   Go to page 124 and do Activity 8 with your child.

Exercise 13

Read the paragraph. Then fill in the bubble that best completes each sentence.

The price for an ice cream cone is posted in a shop window. You decide to buy one. "Would you like a topping?" asks the clerk. You decide to have one. The price of your cone has just gone up. A new word for this practice is *shrouding*. Economists think that shrouding affects much of what people buy today.

Ice Cream Cones
$1.50—Maybe

In a restaurant people pay extra for bottled rather than tap water. A new car has many features that add to its cost. If you buy tickets for an event over the phone, there is an additional charge. How can a consumer avoid shrouding? One answer is to think carefully about the value of things before buying.

1. From this paragraph you can conclude that
   - ○ A. all ice cream cones are the same price.
   - ○ B. prices of things are higher than people realize.
   - ○ C. it's better to drink bottled water than tap water.
   - ○ D. it's worthwhile to order tickets over the phone.

2. From the paragraph you cannot tell
   - ○ A. how shrouding adds to the price of things.
   - ○ B. where the word *shrouding* came from.
   - ○ C. how the cost of a new car increases.
   - ○ D. why a consumer should think carefully.

To parents   Go to page 124 and do Activity 8 with your child.

Point of View

As your child encounters an increasing variety of texts, she needs to be able to go beyond distinguishing fact from opinion. She also needs to be able to sort these facts and opinions to determine the writer's point of view. A reader who is able to recognize the writer's point of view and intention is better able to shape her own point of view and respond to what she reads. The passages and questions in this section will help your child learn to determine the point of view of the writer.

The point of view of an expert, based on knowledge and experience, is often valuable, while viewpoints based on firsthand experience or from an eyewitness often offers new insights into a situation. This section will provide opportunities for your child to consider different points of view and broaden her understanding of a subject.

The extension activities provide additional challenges to your child to encourage and develop her understanding of the particular comprehension skill.

Date: _____

Exercise 1

Read the paragraph. Answer the questions.

Gerardus Mercator, born in 1512, is known for a kind of map. His map—called a Mercator Projection—has caused unfair distortions of the world. For example, the Northern Hemisphere on a Mercator map dominates the world. Greenland appears as big as Africa. Yet Greenland is much smaller than the African continent. North America appears much larger than South America. No doubt, the overblown proportions of places on the map have made people there think of themselves as more important, too.

1. What is the writer's opinion of the distortions on Mercator's map?

   _____

2. Which word in the passage is a clue to how the writer feels about the map's proportions?
   ○ A. smaller   ○ B. larger   ○ C. overblown

3. Which phrase best reflects the writer's point of view?
   ○ A. Admires the mapmaker Gerardus Mercator
   ○ B. Blames Mercator for distorted worldviews
   ○ C. Supports the domination of the Northern Hemisphere

4. What point of view might someone living in Greenland have? _____

   _____

   _____

To parents Go to page 124 and do Activity 9 with your child.

Exercise 2

Read the paragraph. Answer the questions.

France has long been known as a country where people are devoted to their dogs. At some Paris hotels, this is no exception. They offer many services just for the canine set. For example, there are trained dog groomers, charming dog toiletries, and even custom-made beds for pampered pets. These wonderful hotels also provide round-the-clock room service for dogs, with a choice of healthy meals. Of course, dogs are welcome in the hotel restaurants, too. They can't get in without their owners, though!

1. What is the writer's opinion of the treatment of dogs in France? _____

   _____

2. Which word in the passage is a clue to how the writer feels about the hotel services?

   ○ A. wonderful   ○ B. healthy   ○ C. exception

3. Which phrase best reflects the writer's point of view?

   ○ A. Approving of the dog treatment

   ○ B. Upset with the hotels

   ○ C. Outraged about so much attention being given to dogs

4. What point of view might someone who can't make ends meet have?

   _____

   _____

To parents   Go to page 124 and do Activity 9 with your child.

Exercise 3

Read the paragraph. Answer the questions.

Marjory Stoneman Douglas was the heroine of the Everglades, a unique environment in Florida. Many animals make their home in this wetland region. Nevertheless, for years the Everglades were being drained off for buildings and roads. The water was polluted. So Douglas wrote a book, *The Everglades: River of Grass.* In it she explained why the Everglades were important and should be protected. In 1969, Douglas started an organization called Friends of the Everglades. The Friends kept an airport from being built there!

1. What is the writer's opinion of Marjory Stoneman Douglas? _____
_____

2. Which word in the passage is a clue to how the writer feels about the Everglades?
   - ○ A. polluted   ○ B. home   ○ C. unique

3. Which phrase best reflects the writer's point of view?
   - ○ A. Annoyed by the work of Douglas
   - ○ B. Uninterested in the fate of the Everglades
   - ○ C. Impressed by the efforts of Douglas

4. What point of view might a builder have about Marjory Stoneman Douglas?
_____
_____

To parents Go to page 124 and do Activity 9 with your child.

Exercise 4

Read the paragraph. Answer the questions.

Scientists say that nature is really amazing. Recently, some scientists were studying a strange sponge found deep in the Pacific Ocean. They insisted that filaments on the sponge were much like optical fibers used in telecommunication systems. Their somewhat dubious plan was to study the sponge with the hope of duplicating its features for future uses. What those uses are, the scientists haven't said. Stay tuned!

1. What is the writer's opinion of nature? _____
_____

2. Which word in the passage is a clue to how the writer feels about the scientists' plan of study?
   ○ A. dubious   ○ B. amazing   ○ C. hope

3. Which phrase best reflects the writer's point of view?
   ○ A. Awed by scientists and nature
   ○ B. Skeptical about the sponge study
   ○ C. Excited about the sponge project

4. What point of view might a scientist in the study have? _____
_____
_____

To parents Go to page 124 and do Activity 9 with your child.

Exercise 5

Read the paragraph. Answer the questions.

Poor spellers shouldn't try to sell things through online ads. Suppose you want to sell a camera on eBay, but your ad says "Camra for Sale." Buyers looking for cameras aren't likely to find your ad. However, some clever buyers are on the lookout for misspelled ads written by careless sellers. When they find one, they offer a low bid. Since no one else is bidding for the item, the seller often lets the item go for a low price. Often, the smart buyers then turn around and sell the item for more—through an ad that's spelled correctly!

1. What is the writer's opinion of buyers who look for misspellings?

   _____

2. Which word in the passage is a clue to how the writer feels about sellers who misspell?

   ○ A. clever   ○ B. careless   ○ C. smart

3. Which phrase best reflects the writer's point of view?

   ○ A. Sympathetic to spelling problems
   ○ B. Disappointed by poor spelling
   ○ C. Impatient with poor spellers

4. What point of view might a poor speller have? _____

   _____

   _____

To parents   Go to page 124 and do Activity 9 with your child.

Exercise 6

Read the paragraph. Answer the questions.

I was awakened from a deep sleep the other morning by the awful noise of a car alarm. It was the kind that goes off in an unpleasant, repetitive way every few minutes. Finally, someone came and drove the offending vehicle away. The next morning, I awoke to the same annoying sound. When I looked out the window, there was no car. All I saw was a mockingbird on my fence. And sure enough, that remarkable bird was imitating a car alarm. I have to admit it was quite a performance.

1. What is the writer's opinion of car alarms? _____
   _____

2. Which word in the passage is a clue to how the writer feels about the mockingbird?
   ○ A. offending   ○ B. repetitive   ○ C. remarkable

3. Which phrase best reflects the writer's point of view?
   ○ A. Joyful enthusiasm
   ○ B. Reluctant admiration
   ○ C. Bored

4. What point of view might the neighborhood cat have? _____
   _____
   _____

To parents Go to page 124 and do Activity 9 with your child.

Exercise 7

Read the paragraph. Answer the questions.

Watch out for wet dogs. They shake water all over and often smell funny. Many people attribute this smell to a dog's fur. However, a strong odor from a wet dog is more likely to be caused by a skin problem, not wet fur. Some dogs such as cocker spaniels and terriers get rashes and skin irritations that result in body odor. Water can make the odor more noticeable. According to dog experts, the best way to prevent smelly dogs is by grooming them regularly.

1. What is the writer's opinion of wet dogs? _____
_____

2. Which word in the passage is a clue to how the writer feels about the odor of wet dogs?

   ○ A. funny   ○ B. grooming   ○ C. attribute

3. Which phrase best reflects the writer's point of view?

   ○ A. Worried about wet dogs

   ○ B. Interested in helping dog owners

   ○ C. Delighted by dog smells

4. What point of view might a cat lover have? _____
_____

To parents   Go to page 124 and do Activity 9 with your child.

Exercise 8

Read the paragraph. Answer the questions.

Do dolphins and people have a special relationship? Over the centuries, many civilizations have told stories of bonds between people and these incredible creatures. In an ancient Greek story, the god Dionysus changes some pirates into dolphins. An Australian myth tells about a hero named Gowonda who turned into a helpful dolphin. In a tale from Peru, a pink dolphin sometimes becomes a human. Even today, people report stories of dolphins helping swimmers or guiding ships through dangerous seas.

1. What is the writer's opinion of dolphins? _____

_____

2. Which word in the passage is a clue to how the writer feels about dolphins?
   ○ A. incredible   ○ B. pink   ○ C. dangerous

3. Which phrase best reflects the writer's point of view?
   ○ A. Unimpressed by dolphins and their relationship with people
   ○ B. Admiration of dolphins and their relationship with people
   ○ C. Angry about dolphins and their relationship with people

4. What point of view might a sailor have about dolphins? _____

_____

_____

To parents   Go to page 124 and do Activity 9 with your child.

Exercise 9

Read the paragraph. Answer the questions.

Tigers are the biggest members of the cat family. These magnificent cats are solitary animals and need a large territory in which to hunt. They mark their territory with urine so that other tigers are warned away. Tigers track their prey in silence and then pounce for the kill. A tiger can eat 40 pounds of meat in one meal. Unfortunately, tiger habitats have been destroyed in many parts of Asia, their homeland. Scientists think there may be only 3,000 to 6,000 tigers left in the wild. These mighty animals are close to extinction.

1. What is the writer's opinion of the appearance of tigers? _____
   _____

2. Which word in the passage is a clue to how the writer feels about the strength of tigers?
   ○ A. prey   ○ B. solitary   ○ C. mighty

3. Which phrase best reflects the writer's point of view?
   ○ A. Regretful about the loss of tigers
   ○ B. Joyful about the habitat of tigers
   ○ C. Curious about the fate of tigers

4. What point of view might a person living near the tigers' habitat have about tigers? _____
   _____

To parents   Go to page 124 and do Activity 9 with your child.

Exercise 10

Read the paragraph. Answer the questions.

Do you like fruitcake? Strangely enough, some people do like it! They actually think this heavy, sticky cake is good enough to eat. Most people agree that fruitcake is an English holiday tradition. Most people also think that it's better to give a fruitcake than to receive one. In fact, many people who receive fruitcakes as gifts quickly give them away to someone else. One famous writer even went so far as to say that "nobody in the history of the United States has ever bought a fruitcake for himself."

1. What is the writer's opinion of people who like fruitcake? _____
   _____

2. Which word in the passage is a clue to how the writer feels about fruitcake?
   ○ A. good   ○ B. strangely   ○ C. tradition

3 Which phrase best reflects the writer's point of view?
   ○ A. Admiring of fruitcake
   ○ B. Worried about fruitcake eaters
   ○ C. Mocking of fruitcake

4. What point of view might a fruitcake baker have? _____
   _____

To parents Go to page 124 and do Activity 9 with your child.

Date: _____

Exercise 11

Read the paragraph. Answer the questions.

Niagara Falls is known for people who like to, well, go over the edge. The first mindless daredevil was Annie Edson Taylor in 1901. Bobby Leach went over in 1911, breaking not only his jaw but both kneecaps as well. Some of the next attempts didn't fare well at all. While Roger Woodward survived his trip over the falls in 1960, he never meant to go in the first place. He had a boating accident. Two people in one barrel made it over safely in 1989. Two more in a plastic capsule succeeded in 1995. So, who's next?

1. What is the writer's opinion of people who go over Niagara Falls?

   _____

2. Which word in the passage is a clue to how the writer feels about Annie Edson Taylor?

   ○ A. mindless ○ B. survived ○ C. safely

3. Which phrase best reflects the writer's point of view?

   ○ A. Disapproving of these actions

   ○ B. Sorry about these actions

   ○ C. Startled by these actions

4. What point of view might an extreme sports enthusiast have about going over the falls? _____

   _____

To parents   Go to page 124 and do Activity 9 with your child.

Exercise 12

Read the paragraph. Answer the questions.

Diwali is a happy and delightful holiday that is celebrated by Hindus around the world. Diwali is sometimes called the Festival of Lights. Lamps brighten streets, line building rooftops, and shine from windows. Hindus believe that Lakshmi, the goddess of wealth, uses the lamps to guide her way as she comes to bless homes. Diwali also symbolizes the victory of good over evil. For Hindus, this holiday is the beginning of the New Year. People wear new clothes and eat special foods on this very festive day.

1. What is the writer's opinion of Diwali? _____
   _____

2. Which word in the passage is a clue to how the writer feels about Diwali?
   ○ A. evil   ○ B. festive   ○ C. shine

3. Which phrase best reflects the writer's point of view?
   ○ A. Fearful about this holiday
   ○ B. Enthusiastic about this holiday
   ○ C. Indifferent to this holiday

4. What point of view might an electrician have about this holiday? _____
   _____
   _____

To parents Go to page 124 and do Activity 9 with your child.

Exercise 13

Read the paragraph. Answer the questions.

Streets were a mess in 1923. Not only that, they were downright dangerous. Cars drove through intersections without stopping. So did horse-drawn carriages and bicyclists. Lots of accidents happened, and many people were injured. Then Garrett Morgan invented the electric traffic signal. What a difference! Now drivers knew when to proceed or stop. Morgan's ingenious invention, one of many he made in his lifetime, was the beginning of the traffic light system we use today. This inventor should be thanked!

1. What is the writer's opinion of the traffic light? _____
_____

2. Which word in the passage is a clue to how the writer feels about this invention?

   ○ A. dangerous   ○ B. electric   ○ C. ingenious

3. Which phrase best reflects the writer's point of view?
   ○ A. Weary of Garrett Morgan
   ○ B. Admiring of Garrett Morgan
   ○ C. Uncertain about Garrett Morgan

4. What point of view might a car manufacturer have about this invention?

_____
_____

To parents Go to page 124 and do Activity 9 with your child.

Extension Activities

Activity 1: Charting the Main Idea and Details

Skill: Identifying Main Ideas and Details and Summarizing

Choose a variety of non-fiction texts. Read through each text with your child. Then, ask your child to form a chart for each paragraph and identify the main idea and the supporting details for each paragraph. When she is done, have your child write a short summary of the entire text using the main ideas (and some of the supporting details) for the various paragraphs.

Activity 2: Prediction Table

Skill: Making Predictions

Read a story together with your child stopping before important events in the story. Have your child predict what might happen next and fill in the prediction table. Remind her that predictions are good guesses that are based on evidence from the story and what the characters say or do. Continue reading the story and have your child confirm or change her predictions as you go along.

My Prediction Table		
My Predictions	Evidences	Changes to my Predictions

Activity 3: Fact or Opinion

Skill: Identifying Fact and Opinion

Select a variety of sentences that include facts and opinions. Write a fact or an opinion on a slip of paper each and put them in a bag. As you draw out each slip of paper, have your child identify if the sentence is a fact or opinion. Remember to get her to explain why she thinks a sentence is a fact or opinion.

Activity 4: Fiction and Non-fiction

Skill: Comparing and Contrasting

Pick a topic your child is interested in such as a particular animal or a particular vehicle. Then, choose a non-fiction and a fiction book about the same topic. For example, if your class is interested in cars, then she could read a story about McQueen and a nonfiction book about race cars. Have your child compare and contrast the books. How are the books alike? How are they different? Have your child write her ideas down in a Venn diagram.

Activity 5: Clueing in

Skill: Using Context Clues

You can either use the passages in the book or choose new texts with a few words that your child is unfamiliar with. Remember not to choose texts that are too difficult. Then read through the texts with your child. Identify the difficult words. Work with your child to sift out the clues within the text that may give an idea of what the word means. Remind your child that when she comes across a difficult word, she can use the same method to help her understand the text.

Activity 6: Silent Movie

Skill: Summarizing

Choose a variety of texts. These could be magazine articles or even a chapter in a storybook. Read through the text with your child. Ask your child to identify the important points in the article or the main turning points in a chapter. It is important to work with your child to pick out the salient points and identify the details that are unnecessary to give a gist of the story. Ask your child to summarize verbally what the article or chapter is about. You may even want to take this further and have your child write out the salient points. Sometimes, the points may be combined and further summarized.

Activity 7: Silent Movie

Skill: Inference

Let your child understand that we are often not told explicitly how a person feels. We infer a person's feelings or what is happening around us based on what we see. Watch a muted movie with your child. Have her jot down what she thinks the characters are feeling by observing the characters' actions, body language and facial expressions. Watch the movie again with your child. This time have the volume turned up so that your child can see if she has inferred correctly.

Activity 8: What's in a Bag?

Skill: Drawing Conclusions

Choose a few occupations / scenarios. If you chose an occupation, describe the objects that a particular professional might use and ask your child to guess the occupation and state the clues that she used to draw her conclusions. Alternatively, if you chose a scenario, you can describe the activities that are happening and ask your child to state what she has concluded from what you described and what evidence she has based her conclusion on.

Activity 9: The Viewfinder

Skill: Determining Point of View

Choose a few articles that present two different sides to an argument. Such articles are commonly found in newspapers, on the internet or in magazines. Ask your child to read through the articles and identify the differing points of view that are being presented in the article. Ask her to write them down in a chart. Finally, take this one step further by asking her if she can determine what the writer's point of view is. It is important to remind your child that while many of these articles may present two different viewpoints, often, the writer's viewpoint is also present.

Answer Key

Page 7

1. A   2. B

Page 8

1. B   2. D

Page 9

1. D   2. C

Page 10

1. C   2. D

Page 11

1. C   2. B

Page 12

1. C   2. B

Page 13

1. D   2. A

Page 14

1. A   2. B

Page 15

1. C   2. A

Page 16

1. D   2. B

Page 18

1. B   2. C

Page 19

1. C   2. B

Page 20

1. B   2. A

Page 21

1. A   2. C

Page 22

1. C   2. B

Page 23

1. B   2. C

Page 24

1. A   2. C

Page 25

1. C   2. C

Page 26

1. B   2. A

Page 27

1. C   2. A

Page 29

1. A. Fact   B. Fact   C. Opinion
2. The more important the official, the fancier the wig.
3. After all, it is ridiculous.

Page 30

1. A. Fact   B. Opinion C. Fact
2. Each March and April, strong tides from the Atlantic Ocean push into the Amazon Basin.
3. Surfing for miles up the river is much more fun than a short ocean ride.

Page 31

1. A. Fact   B. Opinion C. Fact
2. He lived in the 16th century in Italy.
3. That was an excellent time for talented people.

Page 32

1. A. Opinion B. Fact   C. Opinion
2. Cats have been around for a long time too.
3. They're not as satisfying as dogs and cats, though.

Page 33

1. A. Fact   B. Opinion C. Fact
2. In Korea, people mark a child's first birthday with a celebration called *tol*.
3. I think cake and ice cream are better.

Page 34

1. A. Opinion B. Fact C. Opinion
2. The guides dress as people did during each period.
3. You'll enjoy this place.

Page 35

1. A. Opinion B. Fact C. Fact
2. The globe is housed in a three-storey glass building there.
3. It's very impressive.

Page 36

1. A. Fact B. Opinion C. Fact
2. These are daily patterns known as circadian rhythms.
3. People should get rid of dandelions because they're weeds.

Page 37

1. A. Fact B. Opinion C. Opinion
2. A version of this game is still around today.
3. Whoever invented it must have been very clever.

Page 38

1. A. Opinion B. Fact C. Fact
2. You can even send pictures in them.
3. More people should use emails to communicate.

Page 40

1. A 2. B
3. They have always been good neighbors.

Page 41

1. B 2. A
3. They have large, complex brains and generate sound waves to help them navigate in the water.

Page 42

1. C 2. A
3. Mozart was born in Austria while Beethoven was born in Germany.

Page 43

1. C 2. A
3. Hay fever is an allergic reaction to pollen while hives are caused by an allergic reaction to certain foods.

Page 44

1. A 2. C
3. Minstrels traveled around the country while jesters usually stayed in the same place and served the same lord.

Page 45

1. C 2. B
3. They are both winged insects and have a pair of antennae.

Page 46

1. A 2. C
3. Missiles and bombs can be fired from a long distance and cause a lot of damage.

Page 47

1. A 2. A
3. Fables and fairy tales are stories enjoyed by people throughout the ages.

Page 48

1. B 2. B
3. They are both ferocious animals.

Page 49

1. C 2. B
3. Kangaroos are bigger and taller.

Page 51

1. B 2. C

Page 52

1. A 2. A

Page 53

1. C 2. C

Page 54

1. C 2. B

Page 55

1. B 2. A

Page 56

1. A 2. B

Page 57

1. A 2. B

Page 58

1. B 2. C

Page 59

1. A 2. A

Page 60

1. C   2. B

Page 61

1. C   2. C

Page 62

1. B   2. C

Page 63

1. A   2. B

Page 64

1. A   2. B

Page 66

1. It had no tail.   2. It was wrecked near the Isle of Man.
3. The Isle of Man   4. C

Page 67

1. Words which are combinations of two or more words.
2. From both words it comes from   3. *Glimmer / motel*
4. B

Page 68

1.The Swedes   2. They were made of notched logs carefully fitted together without nails.   3. There was plenty of lumber.   4. D

Page 69

1. The first seeing-eye dog in the U.S.   2. A blind American   3. A school to train guide dogs   4. A

Page 70

1. High fences can block the view of motorists.
2. They are unattractive or made of ugly material.
3. By blocking views, light or airflow.   4. D

Page 71

1. They refer to the unfortunate in society.   2. Cargo from a wrecked ship.   3. Cargo thrown overboard to lighten the load or keep the goods from sinking.   4. B

Page 72

1. Three goals scored in a row with no other goals scored by other players.   2. Cricket   3. Sometimes fans passed a hat and took up a collection for the player who scored well.   4. C

Page 73

1. Familiar songs   2. "Battle Hymn of the Republic"

3. "Taps"   4. C

Page 74

1. Motor vehicles   2. A self-propelled vehicle
3. It had coiled springs that made the vehicle move like a wind-up toy.   4.B

Page 75

1. Venomous reptiles   2. Brown, gray or tan with diamond-shaped patches or bands on their bodies.
3. To warn their enemies or to distract prey.   4. C

Page 76

1. Bring the head of Medusa   2. The gods   3. With his sword by looking in the polished shield   4. A

Page 77

1. Studying at the dining room table.   2. They formed a pyramid of six chairs around her.   3. The pyramid of chairs came crashing down on her.   4. A

Page 78

1. The largest humanitarian network in the world
2. To identify and protect people who help victims of war
3. Victims of war   4. A

Page 79

1. When someone forces you to do something which makes you uncomfortable, hurt, afraid or depressed
2. Demand that you lie, cheat, steal or do something dangerous for them   3. Let your teachers or parents know   4. D

Page 81

1. A and B   2. Yes / No / Yes

Page 82

1. C and D   2. No / No / Yes

Page 83

1. A and D   2. No / Yes / Yes

Page 84

1. C and D   2. Yes / No / No

Page 85

1. B, C and D   2. Yes / No / Yes

Page 86

1. A, B and C   2. No / No / Yes

Page 87

1. D   2. Yes / No / No

Page 88

1. C   2. No / Yes / Yes

Page 89

1. A, C and D   2. Yes / No / No

Page 90

1. B and D   2. No / No / Yes

Page 91

1. B, C and D   2. No / Yes / No

Page 92

1. A and D   2. Yes / No / Yes

Page 93

1. C and D   2. No / No / Yes

Page 95

1. C   2. A

Page 96

1. B   2. C

Page 97

1. C   2. B

Page 98

1. A   2. C

Page 99

1. D   2. B

Page 100

1. D   2. B

Page 101

1. A   2. D

Page 102

1. B   2. C

Page 103

1. D   2. C

Page 104

1. B   2. A

Page 105

1. B   2. B

Page 106

1. B   2. C

Page 107

1. C   2. D

Page 109

1. Unfair   2. C   3. B   4. Distorted

Page 110

1. Pampered   2. A   3. A   4. Exorbitant

Page 111

1. Heroine   2. C   3. C   4. Frustrated

Page 112

1. Amazing   2. A   3. B   4. Undecided

Page 113

1. Careless   2. A   3. C   4. Indignant

Page 114

1. Awful   2. C   3. B   4. Threatening

Page 115

1. Cautious   2. A   3. B   4. Disgusted

Page 116

1. Amazed   2. A   3. B   4. Helpful

Page 117

1. Admiration   2. C   3. A   4. Frightening

Page 118

1. Surprised   2. C   3. C   4. Unhappy

Page 119

1. Disapproving   2. A   3. A   4. Thrilling

Page 120

1. Delightful   2. B   3. B   4. Threatening

Page 121

1. Impressive   2. C   3. B   4. Impressed